Angels

UNLOCKING
THE MYSTERY

RANDY SHEPARD, PhD

Angels
by Randy Shepard, PhD

Published by Living Power Publishing
923 NE Woods Chapel Rd #242
Lee's Summit, MO 64064
www.livingpower.com

Printed in the United States of America

ISBN-13: 978-0-692-74197-9
ISBN-10: 0-692-74197-6
Library of Congress Control Number: 2016910895

Front cover picture credit: NASA, ESA and the Hubble Heritage Team (STScI/AURA)
https://www.spacetelescope.org/images/ann0901a/

Table of Contents

Special Thanks

I would like to offer my sincerest appreciation to the following people who have made this book possible:

My daughter, Carissa Giffen, who used her wonderful keyboarding talents to transcribe my messages.

My dear friend and fellow teacher, Dan Hurst, who promoted the idea of this book and hounded me to finish it.

My long-time friend Nikk Thompson for his advice on the book and supplemental subject matter.

My friend, Jim Collier, for providing an initial edit on the book.

My friend, William Cody Bateman, who came up with the cover design.

My parents, Ronald and Beverly Shepard, who have been my greatest fans and have helped shape my love for God.

My other two wonderful children, Lindsey and Micah, and my son-in-law, Benjamin Giffen, who believe in me and the work God has called me to.

My dear grandchildren, Jackson, Peyton, Madison, Mya, and Joshua, who provide grandpa with a lot of unconditional love.

And ultimately my God, who gave me the insight and ability to write this book.

Introduction

There's something special about the character of Missourians like me. If somebody tells us something, we answer, "You'll have to show me." We're not gullible. We need palpable evidence.

But is that always true? Sometimes it's the things we can't see that are the most real. You can't see electricity, but you know it's there. You can't see gravity, but it's very much there. The same is true with the spiritual world. You can't see it, but it's absolutely there.

Many people refuse to believe in things unless science can back it up. However, scientists will all agree on one thing: What they know about our universe and our world is very little compared to what is yet to be known or discovered. While man stands amazed at how far we have come in understanding our world, the truth is we've only just begun. Even today, science cannot answer the most basic of questions in life such as "Why am I here?" and "What's my purpose in life?" People need to realize that science is limited and doesn't hold all the answers.

It amazes me that within the past one hundred fifty years science has advanced exponentially in almost every area of knowledge with the exception of one—our understanding of the spiritual world.

Though untold numbers of people throughout history have believed in angels and testified to their existence through personal contact, still science refuses to investigate these claims. For millions of people around the globe who've experienced the supernatural, they've come to realize there's more going on in this world than what meets the eye. For those who've taken it seriously and come to understand it, it has awarded them with a wisdom that has dramatically influenced their lives.

The fact is clear: we are not alone! How can science turn its head when nearly every major religion in the world points to the reality of angels and the spiritual realm? The Quran speaks of angels and asserts it was the angel Gabriel who gave Mohammad his message. The ancient Torah of Judaism tells numerous stories of angels. Even Hinduism and Buddhism inform their followers about angelic activity in the world, often referring to them as "divas" or "shining ones."

Out of all these religious texts, I can't find a more resourceful study on angels than the Holy Bible. Within its pages, you'll discover nearly three hundred verses referring to angels. These incredible verses provide us with many acute insights—such as who they are, what their purpose is, what they look like, and why they're interested in us. As such, out of all the religious resources bringing to light the subject of angels, the Bible is by far the most comprehensive in explaining who these fascinating beings are. Therefore, I will use the Bible as the primary resource for our study on angels.

Is the Bible Reliable?

After forty years as a student of both science and religion, I've had the pleasure of researching a lot of material in both fields. In fact, I love information. Gaining knowledge in a variety of matters has always been important to me.

I've always had this conviction: if you're going to stand on a stage and teach people life-transformational truths, you need to be a well-rounded, well-balanced, and well-studied individual. Please don't let me mislead you into thinking that I'm a smart guy. The words "smart" and "Randy Shepard" hardly ever go into the same sentence. I was actually the fastest guy in the slow class.

Seriously though, learning has always fascinated me. As such, it's led me to study numerous books about the spiritual world and how this world can have an impact on each of our lives.

My First Encounter with a Skeptic

I remember as a young man in my early twenties being challenged by a very educated agnostic, someone who doubted the existence of God but was willing to admit his uncertainty. I'd just finished speaking at a church in California. He was the last in line to speak with me, and having learned I was raised in a Christian home, he humbly asked me a very valid question, "Don't you feel a little biased in teaching the Bible as the only source of real truth?"

I admit it, I was a little shocked to be asked that question right after a church service. I told him no.

I was unprepared for his next statement. In fact, it changed my thinking and led me down a path of learning for which I'll always be grateful.

He said, "Randy, I realize you were raised up in a Christian family where the Bible was the key to everything you believed. But I wasn't. The fact is, my family scorned religion. My parents thought that anyone who trusted in the Bible as God's Word only did so using it as a crutch. So tell me, how do you know the Bible is the only source of truth? Have you taken the time to read other religious writings? What makes the Bible the only source from which you or anyone else should draw absolute truth?"

He had a valid point, one I would eventually hear many people ask me over the years. Realizing this was a teachable moment for me, I smiled, put my hand on his shoulder, and said, "Thank you. You've made a good point. One that will make me a better teacher and a better student." Even though in my heart I knew the Bible was God's source of absolute truth, I wasn't prepared to defend it. It was at that point I needed to understand why and how the Bible could stand the test for truth.

Since that day, I've made it a lifetime of study to know the Bible in the light of other religious writings and why it stands so distinctively different. Today, there's no doubt in my mind that man's *only* source of absolute truth is the inerrant, infallible, irrefutable Word of God — the Bible.

Here's Why . . .

While many people have tried to rid the world of the Bible, it remains the number one bestseller of all books ever sold. Billions of people over the centuries have testified to its life-transforming power.

In fact, the Bible is a miracle by nature. Think about it. It was written by more than forty authors over a period of some sixteen hundred years, yet it remains consistent in all areas of study — historically, archeologically, scientifically, prophetically, and even etymologically. Its central theme is unshakably consistent as well.

Even though thousands of people have struggled to disprove the Bible's credibility, no one has ever won that debate. Out of the sixty-six books that make up the Old and New Testaments, the main character has always been Jesus Christ. And the main theme has always been about God setting up His kingdom and dwelling in a loving and intimate relationship with man.

Get Ready to Be Transformed!

As you read this book, an unveiling will take place. As you grasp a greater understanding of the spiritual world around you, it will provide you eye-opening clues to what's going on behind the scenes in your world, your marriage, your kids, your work, and your life. Don't you think that has to be one of the most important discoveries in your life?

When you pull back the veil and take a look at what goes on in the spiritual dimension, you'll view things differently in your life. You'll better understand God's wonderful love for you. You'll realize His great desire to protect and guide you through the use of His angels.

As you journey through this book, you'll find yourself becoming more mindful of the spiritual activity taking place on a day-to-day basis.

Equipping yourself with this kind of knowledge allows you to make better adjustments in how you handle situations.

Imagine you're in a car traveling at high speeds through a sharp curve on a back road somewhere. You can almost feel the weight of your body shifting to compensate for the gravitational and centrifugal forces that are pulling on you. As they do, you automatically grab a handle or throw your hands out to adjust for the pull against your body.

In the same way, you can also make the right adjustments in your life against the spiritual forces that are pulling on you. An understanding of the spiritual activity going on around you can mean the difference between a great marriage and a broken marriage. It can also mean the difference between living a life of peace or one of fear.

This is why God has provided you with so much information about the spiritual world. He knows firsthand how much of an impact it can have on you. It's all around you. This unseen world contains beings that work every day with you in the center of their purpose.

Even though these spiritual beings can interact with us, God is the ultimate authority over all of these beings. They don't do anything without His knowledge. And they can't do anything without His permission. Remember, God's plan for you is a life of victory! As such, He's given you authority over the spiritual world through faith in Him and His name.

Today, I urge you to open your eyes to see what God so desperately wants you to know. Find success. Take control. Be happy. Make your marriage successful. Enjoy life to its fullest. All of this can be yours when you understand the spiritual world and the power God extends to you to control it.

Please understand this book is not about glorifying angels at all. It's really about glorifying the God who made them. It is about understanding exactly why He tells us about them and what He wants us to know about them.

The first step to living the kind of wonderful life God intended for us to have is to realize a very important fact: we're not alone!

Chapter 1

We're Not Alone!

In 1870, a small college in Indiana was hosting the National Methodist Minister's Conference. The college president was asked to open the ceremony. He was quite the visionary. As he addressed ministers who came from all over the United States, he prophetically proclaimed, "We're living in an exciting age. I think that we're going to see things happen in our lifetime that right now are just unbelievable!"

One of the ministers close to him asked, "What do you see? What kinds of things do you mean?"

The president replied, "Well, all kinds of things. I believe we're coming into a time of great inventions. Why, I believe, for example, that one day we'll be able to fly through the air like birds!"

Shocked by what he heard, the minister shouted back, "You what? You believe that one day we'll be able to fly?"

"Yes, sir, I do," said the college president.

"Why, that's heresy! Just heresy," the minister responded. "The Bible says flight is reserved for the angels and for the angels alone. We'll have no such talk here."

Feeling mortified by such absurdity coming from the college president, the young Methodist minister grabbed his two sons, Orville and Wilbur, and stormed out of the conference.

From that conference, however, the seeds of possibility were planted in two young minds. Several years later, in December 1903, Orville and Wilbur Wright built and flew the first successful airplane, believing in the idea that man could one day fly like the birds. What seemed to be an absolute impossibility in 1870 became a reality a few decades later.

Today, flying at speeds beyond 500 mph at 36,000 feet above sea level is just a way of life for millions of people around the globe every day. While few people in the late 1800s believed men would one day fly, most people believed in angels.

Not much has changed since 1870. Most people still believe in angels. In fact, a 2013 survey by the Associated Press found that nearly eight out of ten Americans believe in angels. Through that same study we've also learned that millions more in countries all around the globe believe in angels.

What may seem to be a delusional idea among skeptics and many within the scientific community is actually a fact. The truth is, we're not alone in this world. Millions of testimonials, stone carvings, and ancient texts all over the world tell of the interaction people have had with angels. In fact, nearly every major religion in the world teaches that angels or some form of angels are real.

It's my hope that as you learn more about angels as presented to us in the Bible, it will plant seeds of possibilities in your mind—much as it did for Orville and Wilbur. In other words, you'll become much more mindful to what's going on around you and how angels can impact your life. In the Bible, you'll see how angels dramatically changed the life of many men and women at various time periods and in different settings. Through those stories you'll see how their knowledge of the angels replaced fear with peace. You'll also see how it gave them tremendous confidence to stand strong in the face of overwhelming adversity.

It's amazing to me that while our scientific world will make every attempt to secure billions of dollars in grants to determine if there's alien life outside our planet, no money is spent to better understand those beings who interact with us on a day-to-day basis. Whether you want to believe it or not, a spiritual realm exists.

God has provided us a lot of information about angels. Therefore, He must want us to know about them.

By the end of this book, you'll understand exactly what God says about the unseen world and how it can affect your life from day to day. You'll learn what to believe and what not to believe. You'll understand the powers of the unseen world, what interest those spiritual powers have in you, how they can help you or even hurt you. You'll see just how complex and busy they are, how they influence world leaders, and how they use these leaders to either instigate or avert wars. You'll also realize just how mighty and powerful these spiritual beings are and the tremendous impact they have on the forces of nature.

What about Science and Angels?

I love science. And I love staying on top of new scientific breakthroughs. However, in my study of science I've learned that just because you can't see something doesn't mean it doesn't exist.

More than three centuries ago, Sir Isaac Newton introduced to the world two great laws. One of those laws was gravity. While you might be able to feel gravity's effect under certain circumstances, for most practical purposes you can't feel it, see it, smell it, taste it, or even hear it. Gravity lies outside the parameters of our five senses. And even though it does, no one questions its existence.

About two centuries later, the world of science realized other forces in our universe exist. They found that these forces exceeded well beyond the constraints of our physical senses as well. They called these new discoveries "electromagnetic waves."

Although we can't see, hear, feel, taste, or touch electromagnetic waves, they are bouncing around us and going through our bodies each and every day. Whether they are in the form of radio waves, television waves, microwaves, or cell phone waves, they saturate our world unnoticeable to the senses. To some extent, these waves can even be harmful to us. Still, we believe in them and enjoy their existence and benefits when we turn on a radio, the TV, or search the Internet.

Sadly, science is still in its early stages. Even though it has made some great discoveries in the last two hundred years, it has yet to acquire the ability to measure the spiritual world. Until then, many scientists will refuse to accept the spiritual world in spite of all the evidence. Even though it knowingly inches closer and closer to proving the existence of God, I believe many fear what they might find.

Since science has advanced the frontiers of its knowledge in nearly every direction in the past few years, there are many well-known scientists who've admitted that some things simply can't be explained by physical and natural forces. Nobel Prize-winning neuroscientist John Eccles wrote, "Science cannot explain the existence of each of us as a unique self, nor can it answer such fundamental questions as: Who am I? Why am I here? How did I come to be at a certain place and time? What happens after death? They are all mysteries that are beyond science."

When scientists admit the answers to life's biggest questions lie beyond the scope of science, it no longer seems so naive and unscientific to believe there is a spiritual world. To believe in nonphysical beings—souls or spirits without bodies or brains— may seem delusional to many people, but there are scholars who take angels and demons (fallen angels) seriously. Just because you can't see them or feel them doesn't mean they're not real.

This Really Happened!

I remember in high school during the late 1970s, a very cocky kid named Charlie saw my Bible sitting on top of my school books in my study hall class. With a smirk on his face, he slowly made his way over to my table and said, "Hey...I see your Bible there. I'd like to challenge you on the existence of God."

A little stunned by his statement, I responded, "Oh, really? Okay! What's on your mind, Charlie?"

"Well, Randy, God isn't real, and I can prove it," he said.

"Okay, Charlie, this sounds interesting."

Like an attorney questioning his next witness, he began asking, "Have you, at any time in your life, seen God?"

I immediately thought of that verse that says, "The heavens proclaim the glory of God. The skies display his craftsmanship" (Psalm 19:1). But, realizing that's not what Charlie wanted to hear, I said, "No, I've never seen God."

He smiled and then proceeded with his second question, "Have you ever heard God at any time?"

As he asked that question I immediately thought of all the times I'd heard God speak to my heart or mind about things, but again, realizing this was not what Charlie was asking, I said, "No, I've not audibly heard God."

Feeling confident he was going to win his case, he proceeded with question three, four, and five, "Randy, have you ever felt God, smelled God, or even tasted God at any time?"

I chuckled as he asked me those questions but looked him right in the eye and said, "No, Charlie, none of those."

He once again beamed with his arrogant smile and slapped a friend on the shoulder as though he had made his point. "See, based upon the five senses, I've successfully refuted any basis for the existence of God."

I thought about his statement for a moment while a few of his friends looked on and wondered how I could escape that argument. Then I remembered a speaker I had heard a few years earlier who was faced with the very same question from a friend and how he responded. It's amazing how God will remind you of things at the right time!

Now it was my turn to smile. I looked at him and asked, "Okay, Charlie, now let me ask you a few questions using your same line of reasoning."

He said okay, feeling confident there was no way for me to win this argument.

I looked at the circle of friends who had started to gather around our little discussion and asked him, "Charlie, have you ever at any time seen your brain?"

He paused for a few seconds as he tried to figure out where I was going with this line of questioning. He then replied, "No."

I proceeded with the next question, "Charlie, have you heard your brain?"

He said no.

I then proceeded with questions three, four, and five. "Charlie, have you ever smelled your brain, felt your brain, or even tasted your brain?"

Charlie looked like a kid who had just been caught with his hand in the cookie jar. Without giving him a chance to say anything else, I quickly added, "Charlie, I guess we can all assume that, using the five senses as a basis for all scientific fact to the existence of something, YOU have no brain!"

About ten guys busted out laughing. Charlie was stunned. Quite honestly, he looked a little confused. Wow, did the group ever love that one!

Just because you can't see the spiritual world doesn't mean it's not real.

You Need to Dive beyond the Surface

I'll never forget my first scuba dive into the crystal clear waters of the Caribbean. It was an eye-opener for me. Nothing could have prepared me for what I was about to see.

Not until I stepped off the boat did I realize just how ignorant I was of that world—a world that covers two-thirds of our planet. I knew it was full of life, but I never really gave much thought to just how busy and purposeful life was beyond the surface.

As I descended to 100 feet below the surface, I couldn't believe how clear the water was. Within minutes we were hovering over a shipwreck at 104 feet below the surface. Everywhere I looked thousands of creatures moved in concert with the ebb and flow of the undercurrents of the ocean.

Then it dawned on me. I wasn't looking into an aquarium. I was in it. It was the greatest aquarium on earth. Overtaken by my emotions, I began to cry—something you don't want to do 100 feet below the surface. I was in awe. The ocean was alive and active. Countless numbers of brightly colored fish filled the ocean, along with large beautiful sting-rays, gliding sea turtles, and a coral reef buzzing with life. There they were, slowly going about their day being busy with whatever they do.

As I gained neutral buoyancy a few feet above a coral reef, I became completely surrounded by a school of fish. Hundreds of them moved around me as though I were some kind of fixed structure on the reef. They seemed to have some place to go. Where? I don't know.

Yet one thing I did know was that everything down there was preoccupied with something to do. They all had purpose. After the dive, I found out I could purchase a DVD of the dive from the dive shop. So guess what I did? Yep, I bought it. Every time I pull that video out and push it into my DVD player, I'm awestruck by how active and full the ocean is. In fact, I'm not only amazed by everything I saw, but I'm also stunned by everything I didn't see. There was just so much life down there. You literally could not take it all in. It's too vast.

If I hadn't purchased the DVD, I would have never been able to realize 80 percent of what I didn't see. When you're down there, the ocean is teeming with life all around you. You simply can't capture it all with your conscious mind.

By the same token, if we could somehow dive "beyond the surface" of our physical domain and peek into the unseen spiritual world, we would be absolutely awestruck with the life that goes on around us on a daily basis.

Just like the ocean world, the spiritual world is busy too. The Bible and many other religious books teach us that spiritual beings within the spiritual world are busy fulfilling a mission in concert with a purpose that has you and me as its primary target.

Thankfully, in the ocean I wasn't a target of interest. I've witnessed sharks and large number of barracudas on many dives that, if they wanted to, could have finished me off in seconds. Fortunately, they never seemed to be too interested in my presence.

In the spiritual world, you aren't so lucky. You are a target of interest.

As you read further, you'll understand why. You'll also understand what kind of beings are out there, how these spiritual beings operate, what their purpose is, and why they're so interested in you. You'll even discover what they look like and the limits of what they can and cannot do. Gaining an understanding of the spiritual world can dramatically change your life. It will cause you to be more mindful of what's going on around you every day.

So let's dive beyond the surface and get a better look at the spiritual world around us.

Debunking Common Myths about Angels

One of my major reasons for writing this book is to address the many misconceptions people have about angels. Well-meaning artists and the entertainment world of Hollywood have skewed millions of minds into a concept of angels that vastly differs from what we find in the Bible and many of the other religious texts. With the Bible as our guide, I think you'll be surprised by what you didn't know and how much Hollywood and the Bible differ in their concepts about angels.

Of the many misconceptions people have about angels, here are what I would consider the top four. Many other misconceptions will be addressed throughout the book.

- **Myth – Angels appear in female form.** Unfortunately, many well-meaning artists have depicted angels as having a female gender with flowing long blonde hair. The truth is, there isn't one place in the Bible where you'll find an angel in female form. In fact, every angel in the Bible is always described as looking like a "man." In addition, only masculine personal pronouns such as "he" or "him" are used when referring to an angel.

- **Myth – Angels have wings.** While the old movie classic *It's a Wonderful Life* would like us to believe that every time a bell rings an angel earns its wings, it's simply not true. This may be difficult for many people to swallow, but the Bible never describes any angel as having wings. While God has provided us with detail about the wings of the cherubim, the wings of the seraphim, and the wings of other heavenly creatures, not one scripture tells us that angels have wings. I find it interesting that God would go into such detail about the wings of other heavenly creatures, yet omit this striking feature in the description of angels. Granted, they may have wings. However, the Bible does not tell us that.

- **Myth - Angels play harps.** Many people think of angels as being small chubby babies floating around with halos and playing harps. This isn't true either. Angels are powerful beings that have often brought enormous fear to those who've encountered them. They are anything but cute, and it's never been recorded in any religious texts that they play harps. The only time the Bible refers to harps being played is by another group of beings — not angels.

- **Myth - We become angels after we die.**
  Some people believe that when we die we
  become angels in heaven. However, the
  Bible is clear that this isn't the case at all.
  Angels were created before the creation of
  man. They were created as a one-time act
  of God and for the purpose of serving God
  in His relationship with man. The Bible
  tells us God has other plans for those who
  enter heaven, and it's not that of becoming
  an angel. In fact, when compared to what
  God has planned for mankind in heaven,
  there's no reason why anyone would want
  to become an angel.

These are just a few of the many misconceptions
we'll debunk as you read along.

So What's the Real Truth about Angels?

We've already established that angels play a
prominent role in the teachings of nearly every
major religion the world over, from Islam to
Buddhism to Hinduism to Judaism to Christianity.
Therefore, when you consider all the people who
adhere to these different faiths, it adds up to literally billions of people who believe in the reality
of angels. When you couple that much teaching
going on around the world with the millions of
personal eyewitness accounts, science has a hard
time discounting its reality.

Even today, as the world ponders the $64 billion
question "Does alien life exist?" I believe there's
a larger question at stake—one that is far more

important than the "alien life" question. In fact, I believe it answers the alien life question.

The question is this: "Is there a dimension where living beings exist that have the ability to influence us on a daily basis and reveal themselves to us at various times and in various forms?" After considerable research on this subject over many years, I believe the answer to that question is an unequivocal "Yes!"

Someone once asked me, "Do you believe in UFOs?" I think they were surprised when I said, "Yes, I do."

However, the UFOs that I'm referring to are not the kind you're thinking of. Most people equate UFO sightings with alien life forces. However, when you take a good hard look at the Scriptures, many sightings can be explained by the very fact that we are surrounded by an unseen spiritual world that can appear to us at various times and in various forms.

I've had my own encounter with what many have classified as a UFO. I, however, believe it was a demonic spirit. I'll explain why later, but it's important to know that even the Army Corps of Engineers was called on to investigate this strange phenomenon. After spending several days looking into it, they really couldn't find any conclusion to the matter. It has subsequently been shown on numerous TV shows, including the investigative series *20/20*, but without any real answer as to what the unique UFO-like phenomenon was.

Like that old adage says, "There's more here than what meets the eye." I think that's exactly what the Army Corps of Engineers thought. With all that we've heard in the past and what we hear today about strange and unusual things happening in the lives of people, there's certainly more that goes on in our world than what meets the eye

The world will always have skeptics. Like those who deny the events of the Holocaust in spite of overwhelming evidence. Many people simply choose to hide their heads in the sand rather than face the truth. For those who choose to study this issue in search of real answers about the spiritual world, they won't be disappointed. They'll become a believer in angels like Socrates, who not only confessed in his belief in angels but also admitted he was often influenced by "a good demon."

There is a world of living beings who are very real. They are far more involved in our lives than most of us realize. And, if truth be told, they are more involved than what most of us would care to know.

Please understand my intention is not to scare anyone. Rather, my purpose is to correct many of the misconceptions people have about angels. It's to help you understand more fully who they are, what their purpose is, and why they have so much interest in you.

There's a reason why God has given us so many verses in the Bible about angels. That reason is this: He wants us to know about them and, in turn, understand the enormous love He has for us. He created angels with us in mind. He wants us to know we are not alone.

Three Reasons Why You Should Understand Angels

For simplicity's sake, let me give you three important reasons why you should be motivated to understand the spiritual world and the powerful beings that occupy it.

1. God wants you to know about angels.

I think it immediately stands to reason that God wants us to know about angels. He's put so many verses in the Bible about them. Since God doesn't make mistakes, these verses are in the Bible for a specific reason. While you may not often agree with how God operates or why He allows things to happen, He is perfect in all He does. Psalm 18:30 says, "God is perfect." Consequently, He didn't make a mistake when He placed nearly 300 scriptures in the Bible telling us about angels.

When you examine the Bible closely, you'll discover that more than half the books of the Bible (34 of 66) teach us about angels. In the Old Testament, you'll see 108 verses about angels. In the New Testament, you'll find 187 verses. In fact, no other book of the Bible tells us more about angels than the last book—the book of Revelation. In that one book alone, there are no less than 65 verses discussing angels.

As you study the Bible, you'll see angels performing a variety of things. In the Old Testament, you'll see them speaking to men, protecting men, commanding men, executing judgment upon men, destroying entire cities, praising God, and battling the forces of evil.

In the New Testament, you'll see angels involved in the birth of Christ, the death of Christ, ministering to Christ, talking to Mary and Joseph and many other people. You'll see them freeing Paul from jail, leading men, guiding men, giving instruction to men, and sending judgment upon the earth.

With all the information God gives us about angels throughout the Bible, it becomes very obvious He wants us to know about them. Through these verses God informs us of their appearance, their authority, their actions, their purpose, their abilities, and the interactions they have with us. Yes, God wants us to know about them. And because it's important to Him, it should be important to us!

2. Angels interact with us often.

I don't know about you, but if someone is going to interact with me I'd like to know something about them. Don't you?

That's why you need an understanding of the spiritual world and the spiritual beings who work in that world to influence you. Since the Bible clearly shows that they can interact with us, it only stands to reason that we should know something about them. Doesn't that make sense?

Before I tell you about my own encounter with an angel, let me restate that I believe angels interact with us far more than most of us realize. I think that's the reason why the writer of the book of Hebrews warns his readers:

> Don't forget to show hospitality to strangers, for some who have done this have entertained angels without realizing it!
> —Hebrews 13:2

As I look back on my life, I'm sure there have been many times an angel was at work. I just didn't realize it. It's probably true for you as well. If you could look back at various times and events in your life, you could probably say the same thing. Can you think of some events that may have seemed like a coincidence or a miracle? An angel may have been involved.

I love to hear stories about miracles. Sadly, I've heard too many people recount their miraculous stories only to give "luck" or "fate" the glory. Far too often we fail to realize that luck isn't real and fate is in the hands of God. We often forget there's a God in heaven who loves us more than we can imagine. We neglect to remember how often He enjoys intervening in our lives to protect us and help us. The next time something happens that seems miraculous, don't give luck or fate any glory — give it to God, the One who truly deserves it.

Keep in mind that we have a loving heavenly Father who cares for us and sends His angels to protect and guide us. Luck and fate have nothing to do with miracles. Only God can perform miracles.

As you're reading this book, you might be saying, "Randy, how can I give God the glory when I really don't believe He exists?"

If you feel that way, there are two things I want you to consider. First, if you doubt the existence of God based on the lack of scientific evidence, then you have to throw away luck and fate as well. There is no scientific evidence to support their existence. Secondly, if you give God the glory and realize one day there is no God, then no damage is done. But if you don't give God the glory and one day realize you're wrong, you'll be forever sorry!

For those of you who have a difficult time giving God the glory because of your anger toward Him stemming from some tragedies in your life, you need to find a way to deal with that anger. God loves us deeply, and any anger you harbor against Him doesn't change that fact. When troubling times hit us (and we all face them), we need to remember we don't have the luxury of seeing things from God's perspective. We can't see tomorrow or the next day, or the next year.

God wants us to trust Him in tough times. He wants us to realize that all things in life are ultimately done for our good, especially for those who love Him.

Look at what He said in Romans 8:

> And we know that all things work together for good to those who love God, to those who are the called according to His purpose.
> —Romans 8:28

My First Encounter with an Angel

I almost gave "luck" too much glory one day. It happened during one of the most frightening moments of my life. I was twenty-one years old and driving home from my girlfriend's house when I approached the exit to my hometown. I had forgotten about all the road construction around the exit that day. In those days, the Missouri Department of Transportation didn't possess the high-resolution measures they have today. Therefore, the lanes were much more difficult to see.

As I approached the exit, I noticed that my lane had been altered with a sharp turn to the left—something I didn't expect. In one panicked motion, I grabbed the steering wheel and pulled it hard to the left to avoid hitting a road sign. It only made matters worse.

I not only overcompensated for the turn, but keep in mind I was driving a 1967 Cutlass with no power steering, a bench seat with no seatbelts, and no airbags. This was before laws concerning seatbelts and airbags were written.

Pulling hard left was a mistake. Now I was headed in the direction of a concrete barrier at sixty-five mph. As adrenaline pounded through my veins, I once again turned the steering wheel with a hard right.

Relieved that I had avoided a head-on collision with a concrete barrier, my next concern was careening off the end of a bridge. Now my heart was really pumping. Again I yanked my steering wheel hard left. It took only a few milliseconds to realize I was out of control.

Just before I slammed my car into the concrete wall, I remember praying, "Lord, protect me!"

Bang! The sound of impact was almost deafening. The concrete barriers shattered, and the high pitch of metal screeching to an almost endless tune is something I'll never forget. I didn't realize it at the time, but my car overturned several times down the highway.

As the car continued to roll, my mind kept begging the questions, "When am I going to die? When will I be thrown from my car?" And, "What is that warm embrace I feel around my body?"

When my car finally came to a stop, I ended up slumped down in the middle of the bench seat. Stunned and confused, I wondered, "Am I okay? Did this really happen to me?"

Soon I could hear the blast of sirens blaring from different directions. As I checked my body over, I realized that nothing seemed to hurt. But when I tried to sit up, I felt a sharp pain searing through the middle of my back. My first thought was, "Oh boy! You've really hurt yourself now!"

As emergency crews arrived, I simply laid my head back, closed my eyes, and replayed that horrible wreck in my mind. I recalled praying and asking God for protection before I hit the wall. I also remembered the weird feeling of a warm embrace around my torso as though something were holding me in that car. It felt as though someone or something had a grip around my chest. It had a warm feeling to it. I can't explain it any other way.

The police report said my bumper flew ninety feet. With no seatbelts, I should have followed right behind the bumper or been tossed out the side of the car on one of its barrel rolls.

As emergency crews rushed onto the scene, I remember looking around the car. The roof was caved in. All the windows were shattered. My leather jacket was torn to shreds. The car was so crumpled that even the Jaws of Life couldn't extricate me. Yet somehow I remained unharmed, sitting in the middle of that bench seat.

Emergency crews struggled to find a way to get me out of the car. Finally, they decided to send me out the back window.

I remember a fireman telling me, "Son, you're lucky to be alive!" Many of the policemen who were coordinating all the traffic thought I had died. In fact, a police officer told my dad later that when he drove by the crash site, he didn't know how anyone could have survived a crash like that.

Once out of the car and into the ambulance, I was thoroughly checked over by a couple of EMTs, one of them again reminding me how lucky I was to be alive.

We arrived at the hospital in a matter of minutes. Doctors ran multiple X-rays and found nothing wrong or broken. I did have a few scrapes from flying glass and some sore ribs, but I walked away from that hospital about two hours later.

While waiting for my dad to pick me up at the hospital, I kept wondering how I had escaped such a devastating car crash. I was also wondering, "What was that warm embrace around my body?"

My dad arrived at the hospital a few hours later to take me home. He didn't say much until we stepped into the house from the garage. As we entered the house he turned to me and said, "Son, it's a good thing you're into body building."

Not more than a second passed by and my dad stopped in his tracks. He realized what he had just said. He turned and looked at me and said, "No, son, I take that back. God protected you tonight. God sent His angel to keep you safe."

That was the moment it dawned on me what that warm embrace must have been. It was an angel! I had prayed and asked for God's protection just before I hit the concrete wall. God had sent His angel to protect me and save my life that night.

Several years later, my uncle Dale endured a similar event. His conversion van slipped on an icy spot on the road, causing it to flip several times into an empty field. He too tells the story of how an angel came and held him in one spot while the van went wildly out of control, flipping several times.

His story, unlike mine, has a very interesting twist. Three weeks before his crash, his church voted to donate a car to his family. At the moment of the crash, the pastor was on his way to tell my uncle the good news. When he heard about what had happened, he met Dale at the hospital. After all the tests and X-rays revealed a clean bill of health, the pastor began to laugh.

He said, "Dale, I've got some interesting news for you! The church voted three weeks ago to donate a car to you and your wife, and I was on my way to deliver you the keys today."

God had sent His angel.

If you have an angel story too, I'd love to hear about it! Visit my book's website at:

www.AngelsUTM.com

Tell us your story. The world is waiting to hear it!

3. We receive a huge benefit by understanding them.

Developing an understanding of angels, how they work, and their purpose can provide us with some exciting benefits. One of those major benefits is how you can make good choices and adjustments in your life.

Let me illustrate what I mean through the examples of gravity and electromagnetic waves.

For thousands of years, man has interacted with a variety of things he can't see. Until a few hundred years ago, he didn't even know about them.

One of those is gravity. Everyone knows if you jump up, you're going to come back down. We also know that if we jump off a cliff we'll keep falling until something stops us. Understanding the nature of these forces allows us to make good choices and adjustments.

Another force we can't see is electromagnetic waves. We've discovered they're everywhere! They bounce all around us and go right through us. Until the last 120 years or so, we didn't even know they existed. Today we know a lot about these waves and have developed the right receivers—whether it's a radio, TV, or cell phone—and we enjoy the benefits of that understanding every day.

The benefits to knowing about the spiritual world aren't much different. While it too isn't something we can see, we derive great benefits from understanding the beings that inhabit the spiritual domain, and understanding their ability to interact with us can literally transform our lives.

Let's talk next about how this knowledge can make a difference in your life.

Chapter 2

Why You Should Know about Angels

As a young man, I remember the day the hair stood on the back of my neck when the great evangelist John R. Rice announced to his large audience, "If we could go beyond the surface of the spiritual world and our eyes could be open to what's really going on around us, we'd be amazed at what we'd find! We would see thousands of angels and demons fighting over each of us every day!"

As he shared that riveting thought, my mind raced back to the Scripture verses found in the Old Testament in 2 Kings 6. It's the incredible story of Elisha (the prophet of God) and his servant who, on one unique occasion, was given the rare privilege of having his eyes unveiled to the spiritual world.

The story begins with the army of Aram descending the hillsides to kill Elisha and his servant. What you read next is the reaction of the two men. Elisha was calm and at perfect peace while his servant was trembling in absolute fear. Their reactions couldn't have been more opposite.

Elisha's response to the news of impending disaster was based on his knowledge of God, of His amazing love, and of His willingness to send His angels to protect those who love Him and call on His name for protection.

Elisha's servant, however, was another story. He lacked the knowledge Elisha had. Consequently, like so many of us when faced with impending doom, he was ready to flee in abject terror. As Elisha's servant turned to run, Elisha tried to remind him of an important truth. He said that God would send His angels to protect them from the army of Aram. However, his servant was so blinded and gripped by fear that in that moment he just couldn't reconcile that thought in his mind.

When Elisha realized his words had no positive effect upon his servant, he asked God for a favor. He asked God to open his servant's eyes to the spiritual world. Elisha wanted his servant to understand a spiritual truth about God that he had learned a long time ago. He wanted his servant to learn that God often protects His own through the use of His mighty angels.

That day, God answered Elisha's prayer. He pulled back the veil and opened his servant's eyes to the spiritual realm. The servant was amazed to see thousands upon thousands of angels all over the hillside ready to destroy the army of Aram.

Read this amazing story and then think about what God can do for you.

So one night the king of Aram sent a great army with many chariots and horses to surround the city. When the servant of the man of God got up early the next morning and went outside, there were troops, horses, and chariots everywhere. "Oh, sir, what will we do now?" the young man cried to Elisha. "Don't be afraid!" Elisha told him. "For there are more on our side than on theirs!" Then Elisha prayed, "O LORD, open his eyes and let him see!" The LORD opened the young man's eyes, and when he looked up, he saw that the hillside around Elisha was filled with horses and chariots of fire.

—2 Kings 6:14-17

Benefit #1 – We realize how God operates and how He often uses His angels to protect us.

Elisha knew how God operated. He had a close relationship with Him. That relationship brought about an unswerving faith in God's angelic protection. If this kind of knowledge made a difference for a man like Elisha, what could it do for you?

Sadly, like Jesus's disciples, we often forget about God's amazing ability.

I'm reminded how on the Sea of Galilee one day the disciples were battling a brutal storm. Jesus was fast asleep in the back of the boat. As the storm and winds raged on, His disciples had forgotten who was in the boat with them. They were so focused on their circumstances that they simply forgot about Jesus. How many times has that happened to you?

In spite of all the miracles Jesus had performed right in front of their eyes, they were at the end of their ropes and believed they were about to die. As the thought of imminent death overwhelmed them, Jesus calmly woke from His sleep, spoke to the wind and rain, and amazed His disciples when the elements of nature *obeyed His command.*

Can you imagine how embarrassed His disciples must have been? They knew they had blown it again. Like so many times before, they were so focused on the problem right in front of them that they totally forgot the power of Jesus to save them.

Going back to the story of Elisha, when you read this amazing story, what do you think you should learn from it? God gave us this story so that we would learn more about how He operates and uses His angels in the desperate times we face.

How many times has God placed His angels around you to protect you, but you've neglected to realize it? How many times has fear gripped you because you've focused so heavily upon your circumstances that it's kept you from realizing God's presence and power to deliver you?

When you read stories like this, you have to remember God is recording this story for your benefit. He's reminding you of what He's doing behind the scenes. Reading stories like this throughout the Bible should give you the ability to open your eyes to the truth about God and how He works in your life. Instead of being gripped by fear and dwelling on the troubles in front of you, I want to challenge you to remember Elisha's story and trust in the God who can help you.

Someone once said to me, "Randy, it's not fair! I wish God would let us see what's going on behind the scenes in the spiritual world."

Yes, it would be nice if God would open our eyes to the spiritual world and let us take a peek at what's really going on around us. However, God is trying to build up our faith in Him. He wants us to trust Him in difficult times. He wants us to put all of our faith in Him. He's given us His Bible so that we can read these kinds of stories and learn from them. God's not hiding from us. Through His Word He's trying to reveal Himself to us. He wants us to understand and believe in the amazing love He has for us. After all, He created angels to serve Him for our benefit.

Here are a couple of questions for you.

- If you could exchange the fear that grips you about certain things in your life and replace it with a calming assurance, would that be important to you?
- If you could break the grip that depression, anger, hatred, frustration, and stress has on you and replace it with a hope and peace that calms every fiber of your being, would that benefit you?

This is the kind of benefit I'm talking about. Having an understanding of how God operates in your life through His angels can be very calming and reassuring.

Once you get through this book, you'll be like the servant of Elisha. You'll learn things about God and His mighty angels you never knew before.

Benefit #2 – You'll gain a better understanding of what's really going on in the world.

When you understand angels—who they are, what their purpose is, and how they interact with you every day—you'll have a better understanding of what's going on in the world and what's going on around you.

Have you ever listened to the evening news and said to yourself, "God, what in the world is going on?" Many people have. But when you understand how the spiritual forces work throughout the world, it all seems to make sense. It's not that we completely understand it, but we realize there are unseen forces at work that are using world leaders and even our own coworkers to create an unsettling of events.

The Bible tells us there are powerful spiritual forces at work—both good and evil. As such, it's important to keep in mind that the focus of that battle is over us, the human race. The apostle Paul said in Ephesians:

> For we are not fighting against flesh-and-blood enemies, but against evil rulers and authorities of the unseen world, against mighty powers in this dark world, and against evil spirits in the heavenly places.
> —Ephesians 6:10-12

As we battle things in this physical world, there's also a battle being fought in the spiritual dimension around us. It may not seem fair that we're in a battle with things we can't see, but it happens to be a reality we must deal with. What Paul is saying in these verses is simply a reminder of this important fact.

Even when it comes to contentions at home or at work, the real battle may be more than just a personality clash or differing views. Oftentimes when you're in a battle that can't be easily fixed, that battle may be propelled by spiritual forces determined to distract you, discourage you, frustrate you, and stress you out.

Let me for a moment take this thought up to a higher level. Let me take it into something bigger than just your little world.

Have you ever asked the question, "What possessed so many German Nazis to blindly follow Adolf Hitler in his endeavor to wipe out the Jewish race?"

Maybe you've wondered how men like Saddam Hussein of Iraq, Bashar al-Assad of Syria, or even the leader of the extreme butchers of ISIS, Abu Bakr al-Baghdadi, can coldly exterminate and behead innocent men, women, and children.

The Bible explains it thoroughly! It shows us in Ephesians 6 that our real enemy is not a "flesh and blood" enemy. It's a spiritual enemy.

In fact, the Bible teaches us that there are powerful wicked spirits (evil angels) in high places working in the hearts and minds of world leaders like these men. Under the influence of these evil spirits, such men lose control of themselves and are literally held captive under Satan's will.

One of the most frightening truths of the Bible is Satan's ability to take those who reject God captive at his will. While Adolf Hitler, Saddam Hussein, and many other evil leaders may have thought they were acting on their own volition, in reality they had refused to bow their knee to God and became pawns of Satan. Once held captive by Satan's will, they were doomed to commit horrible atrocities on mankind. Their power came not from their own ability but from the power granted by Satan, the prince of this world.

Perhaps God will change those people's hearts, and they will learn the truth. Then they will come to their senses and escape from the devil's trap. For they have been held captive by him to do whatever he wants.

— 2 Timothy 2:25-26

Now, stepping it down a notch and focusing on your world, though the challenges you face with your boss or coworkers may be stressful and at times extremely depressing, the Bible warns that behind all anger, frustration, and lack of unity there could be an evil spirit that's doing everything possible to create havoc in your life.

The same is true in your marriage and the relationships you have with others. There are wicked spiritual forces at work that may be trying to do everything they can to create stress, frustration, and depression.

Granted, there will always be trials and tribulations that are the byproducts of your own making. Your sinful nature, steeped in selfishness and pride, likes to raise its ugly head from time to time. Many times the secret to living a stress-free life is found in simply defeating the sinful nature you were born with. At other times it's defeating the spiritual forces at play.

That reminds me of a story someone once told me about an old Native American who said, "I feel like I have two dogs within me that are constantly at battle against each other. One of those dogs wants to do well. The other wants to do bad."

The hearer of the story asked the old man, "Who usually wins?"

He replied, "The one I say 'Sic 'em' to."

When it comes to the evil angels working to create an environment or a thought process that leads you down a path to stress, anger, bitterness, and depression, we shouldn't fear. There is good news! Through Jesus Christ, we can overcome these evil powers and find the peace and help God so clearly wants to send our way.

Notice how excited Jesus's disciples were about the power granted them to control the evil spirits through their relationship with Christ:

> "Lord, even the demons obey us when we use your name!" "Yes," he told them, "I saw Satan fall from heaven like lightning! Look, I have given you authority over all the power of the enemy, and you can walk among snakes and scorpions and crush them. Nothing will injure you. But don't rejoice because evil spirits obey you; rejoice because your names are registered in heaven."
>
> —Luke 10:17-18

In reality, it's Jesus who has the power over the spiritual world. Through our relationship with Him and through the power of His holy name we can overcome these evil spirits. Through His death and resurrection He has overcome the world, including the unseen spiritual world. That's why we should live in peace, not in fear!

> "I have told you all this so that you may have peace in me. Here on earth you will have many trials and sorrows. But take heart, because I have overcome the world."
>
> —John 16:33

It's important to keep in mind that there is a battle being fought to either provide you with a satisfying and joyful life, or one that's designed to decimate any joy you may find in life. As Jesus seeks to fill your life with an abundance of joy, Satan (the thief) wants to take it away.

> The thief's purpose is to steal and kill and destroy. My purpose is to give them a rich and satisfying life.   —John 10:10

The good news is, Jesus is "far above all" the forces of evil.

> Now he is far above any ruler or authority or power or leader or anything else—not only in this world but also in the world to come. God has put all things under the authority of Christ and has made him head over all things for the benefit of the church.
> —Ephesians 1:20-22

In spite of the power Satan does possess, he is still under God's control. He's subject to God's power and authority. He was created by God and is unable to do anything without His consent. A great example of this is found in the book of Job.

> Then the LORD asked Satan, "Have you noticed my servant Job? He is the finest man in all the earth. He is blameless—a man of complete integrity. He fears God and stays away from evil." Satan replied to the LORD, "Yes, but Job has good reason to fear God. You have always put a wall of protection

around him and his home and his property.
You have made him prosper in everything
he does. Look how rich he is! But reach out
and take away everything he has, and he will
surely curse you to your face!" "All right,
you may test him," the LORD said to Satan.
"Do whatever you want with everything he
possesses, but don't harm him physically."
So Satan left the LORD's presence.

—Job 1:8-12

Being that God has all authority in heaven and
on earth, we have nothing to worry about.

But you belong to God, my dear children.
You have already won a victory over those
people, because the Spirit who lives in you is
greater than the spirit who lives in the world.

—1 John 4:4

Benefit #3 – They teach us how we should live.

A lot of things are vying for our attention today —
TV, the Internet, music, video games, our jobs, our
kids, and doing everything we can to keep our lives
in balance. Sadly, we get so focused on these things
that we forget the most important thing in life: our
relationship with God.

You see, this is one thing we can learn from
angels. Angels clearly see that God is the only One
who really matters. There's nothing more important in this entire universe than to commit everything they are to Him and for His glory. They have
tunnel vision when it comes to God. Their whole

focus is upon Him. They adore Him, praise Him, love Him, and worship Him.

As we look into the Scriptures, one of the most common things we see is their commitment to follow every one of His commands.

Notice what the psalmist says about angels:

> Praise the LORD, you angels, you mighty ones who carry out his plans, listening for each of his commands. Yes, praise the LORD, you armies of angels who serve him and do his will!　　　　　—Psalm 103:20

Notice how committed they are to God. In this one passage alone, you can see three very important truths about angels:

First, they carry out God's plans. They aren't out there wandering space doing whatever they want to do. They aren't carrying out their plans. Their entire existence and function is dedicated to serving God and His plans. They have no agenda of their own. They do not and will not operate apart from the perfect will and command of God. Isn't this something we should want to do every day?

Secondly, they listen carefully to each of His commands. This too is something we ought to be doing.

Thirdly, they serve God continuously. In other words, they never stop serving God—not for a second. They can't see value in anything else other than God.

This attitude is so opposite of us. Some days we feel like serving God, and other days we don't. Not angels! They serve Him at full capacity with great joy and enthusiasm every moment of every day. Isn't this something we should be doing too?

I'll admit, angels do have an advantage over us. They live in the glorious presence of God. They stand before His throne every day. They know the power He possesses. They had a front row seat when He spoke the universe into existence. They also get to see Him exercise His power in our lives every day.

Can you imagine how incredible and indescribable it must be for the angels to witness God's presence and power on a daily basis? Can you fathom their amazement when they witnessed God's dynamic power at creation? Are you able to imagine how they might have gasped at His majesty when He spoke into the darkness and unleashed the forces of creation in unprecedented magnitude? How thrilling it must have been to see Him command the galaxies to form, along with the billions of stars and planets that fill them.

Today, thanks to the Hubble telescope, we know there are billions of galaxies throughout the incomprehensible vastness of space with each galaxy containing billions of stars and planets.

As I look up into the night sky, I'm often reminded of Psalm 147:4 where the psalmist says, "He counts the stars and calls them all by name."

Imagine that. God has a name for every single star! What an incredible God we serve!

No wonder the angels follow Him, glorify Him, worship Him, and obey each of His commands. In fact, God describes the reaction of the angels at the moment of creation:

"Where were you when I laid the foundations of the earth? Tell me, if you know so much. Who determined its dimensions and stretched out the surveying line? What supports its foundations, and who laid its cornerstone as the morning stars sang together and all the angels shouted for joy?"
                                        — Job 38:4-7

What do you think your reaction would have been?

Just close your eyes and imagine being one of His angels as you listen to God commanding particles to form. Then imagine God speaking with a thunderous shout and feeling and seeing His indescribable power at work as heat, centrifugal force, gravity, and many other forces come together to form the planets and stars far, far larger than any angel could possibly even imagine.

Then try to imagine Him grouping these celestial bodies together in an orchestrated fashion and commanding them to be contained and move through space governed by certain powers. Then imagine yourself watching the Almighty scattering these unfathomable celestial bodies out across the vast darkness of space. No wonder the angels shouted for joy!

Angels are fully aware that God, and only God, is the greatest power in the universe. They know God is their creator.

Sadly, there are many people all over the world who venerate angels. For some odd reason, they want to worship them. Some even pray to them. I believe it's partly due to a serious lack of knowledge about God and His angels.

Those who do pray to angels or worship them need to realize the Bible strongly condemns this action. In fact, there isn't one angel of God who would allow us to pray to them or worship them. Demons will allow it, but God's angels won't.

On one occasion, the apostle John—one of Jesus's disciples—tried to worship an angel. As he stood in the mighty angel's presence receiving the information known as the book of Revelation, he was overcome with emotion and began to worship the angel.

Notice what the angel did. He stopped John immediately and reminded him that there's only one Person worthy of worship—God alone:

> Then I fell down at his feet to worship him, but he said, "No, don't worship me. I am a servant of God, just like you and your brothers and sisters who testify about their faith in Jesus. Worship only God. For the essence of prophecy is to give a clear witness for Jesus." —Revelation 19:10

Here's an important and critical fact that everyone needs to know: the angels of God don't want to be worshipped. They want all attention, glory, honor, and prayer to be directed to God.

In this passage alone, we see the angel saying two very important things. First, he forbids John from worshipping him. He corrects him and tells him not to do it.

Secondly, this mighty angel reminds John that he is merely "a servant" just like him.

Isn't that amazing? Angels who stand in the presence of God do not see themselves as being any better than us. In fact, the angel said he is just like us in that we are all servants of God.

Unfortunately, many people try to place angels on a glorified pedestal. Some people will even go so dangerously far with this view as to equate them with God Himself.

Remember, there isn't one angel of God who wants this. If given the opportunity, they would stop you just as they did John. They would remind you in no uncertain terms that the only one worthy of worship and prayer is God!

This brings me to an important point.

Angels aren't anything like God. While they possess a spirit nature like God, their attributes and abilities are nothing like God's.

Angels aren't all-knowing like God. They aren't all-powerful like God. And they can only be in one place at a time—very much unlike God. The truth is, instead of trying to compare them to God, we should be comparing angels to ourselves. They do!

Remember what the mighty angel said to John? He reminded him, "I am a servant of God, just like you and your brothers and sisters who testify about their faith in Jesus."

Here's another passage of the Bible that compares them to us. Notice what God tells us in the book of Hebrews:

> And furthermore, it is not angels who will control the future world we are talking about. For in one place the Scriptures say, "What are mere mortals [man] that you should think about them, or a son of man that you should care for him? Yet you made

them only a little lower than the angels and crowned them with glory and honor, you gave them authority over all things."

—Hebrews 2:5-8

When God compares angels to man, He describes man as being "a little lower than the angels." Angels are more powerful in strength, more knowledgeable about God's ways, and they can move in and out of the spiritual realm, things we can't do. I think this is what God means when He tells us that we're a little lower than the angels.

Possessing a correct view of angels is important, because having a skewed view can be extremely dangerous. Let's get into the next chapter and look at some of the dangers in not properly understanding angels.

Chapter 3

The Dangers Surrounding Angels

I remember when my kids started driving. My prayer life tripled. I taught all three of my children how to drive, a task I wish upon no one. Each time they'd get behind the wheel (even after they got their driver's license), my wife and I would pray continuously until they got home. Do you know what I mean? Even though the Bible encourages us to "pray without ceasing," we were able to accomplish that feat without any problem.

Have you noticed, or is it just me? It seems like kids have a different set of driving rules. They seem to think the following:

- Turn signals are merely clues about your next move; don't take them seriously.
- The faster you drive through a red light, the less chance of getting hit.
- Braking is to be done hard and late so your anti-lock braking system can kick in.

- Road construction signs are purely suggestions.
- Speed limits are arbitrary figures that simply recommend how fast you should drive before anyone takes them seriously.
- Always slow down and rubberneck when someone is changing a tire.
- Learn to swerve abruptly. It keeps you awake.

Can you relate to that?

Anyway, praying is a good thing, especially when you've got teenage drivers! But when it comes to praying to a higher power, prayer should always go to God and never to an angel. Remember, holy angels only respond to God's command. They don't act on their own volition. They do nothing without God's direct command. So if you want your prayers answered, you've got to direct them to God.

Since the Bible teaches this so clearly, it begs the question, "Why do many people pray to angels?"

I think the answer to that question is probably fourfold. One, they're acting out of ignorance. They simply don't know what the Bible teaches about this subject. Furthermore, they don't understand angels.

Second, I think some people pray to angels because they feel less intimidated by an angel. They may feel God's been too hard to reach in the past, or perhaps He's a little intimidating. Perhaps they feel He is just too transcendent for them to connect with. So some people might feel it's easier to speak with an angel than directly with God.

Third, many people have a skewed or tainted view of God. Some see God as an old man with a white beard who is always angry with us. For people with this view of God, praying to an angel may be the next best thing.

Fourth, some religious teachings actually encourage people to pray to an angel, especially to their guardian angel. However, this is not biblical in any way. This kind of teaching goes against every principle in the Bible (for good reason . . , keep reading!).

In spite of the clear teaching of Scripture on this subject, it amazes me how many books and so-called religious leaders will encourage this type of behavior.

Even WikiHow offers a four-step process on how to contact your angel:

1. Identify your guardian angel.
2. Create an altar.
3. Learn a special prayer.
4. Designate a time to contact your angel.

While this four-step formula might sound reasonable, the Bible never encourages this type of activity at all. In fact, the idea that any of us should in any way communicate with angels is the exact opposite of what God tells us to do!

In the Bible, you'll see several accounts of men and women who have communication with the angels of God. However, in every case you'll notice these common denominators:

- An angel from God always initiates the conversation, not the person.

- An angel from God always announces they are from God.
- An angel from God always comes with a specific message that is clear and concise.
- An angel from God always appears when people least expect it.
- No angel ever forces his message on any person.

While a number of books have been written about communicating with angels, to do so is treading into dangerous territory. Demons are more than happy to communicate with you. They love appearing as though they are angels of God. They want you to believe that they are from God. They are always looking for ways to get into your life. That's why the Bible tells us to "test" the spirits to see if they are really from God!

> Dear friends, do not believe everyone who claims to speak by the Spirit. You must test them to see if the spirit they have comes from God. For there are many false prophets in the world.   —1 John 4:1

Demons are interested in you communicating with them, but God's holy angels aren't. Demons are looking for ways to get into your life, but God's angels are only interested in following God's command as it relates to your life. Remember, they are not looking for any "order" we might give them; they are looking for God's order!

> For he will order his angels to protect you wherever you go. They will hold you up

with their hands so you won't even hurt your foot on a stone. You will trample upon lions and cobras; you will crush fierce lions and serpents under your feet! The Lord says, "I will rescue those who love me. I will protect those who trust in my name.

—Daniel 91:11-13

From this passage, we learn that God does the ordering and the angels do the protecting. But to keep the passage in its proper context, a couple of verses later we learn that it's ultimately God who offers the protection. He simply uses the angels to do His work—much like we do God's work in sharing information about Him and in helping others.

The Bible strictly forbids us from praying to any person or thing other than our heavenly Father. We're not to pray to an angel because they can't act on their own volition. We're not to pray to a saint because they can't hear our prayers, and if they could they would be powerless to do anything without God's consent. In fact, God warns us against praying to anything or anyone other than Him. He calls this an act of idolatry.

Here's a better idea. If you want something, ask God! Jesus told us that all prayer should be directed toward our heavenly Father. I love what Jesus said in the book of John:

You can ask for anything in my name, and I will do it, so that the Son can bring glory to the Father. Yes, ask me for anything in my name, and I will do it!   —John 14:13-14

No angel of God or demon can offer what God can offer you. If we have a God who invites us to ask for things, why do we feel the need to go to an angel? Notice what King David said:

> For you answer our prayers. All of us must come to you.   —Psalm 65:2

While millions of people around the world believe in angels, I've found most of them don't have a clue about the truths surrounding angels. They've never really taken the time to study the subject of angels.

At this point, you know there are two kinds of angels: those who serve God and those who serve Satan. We'll go into greater detail about that later, but the critical thing for you to understand is that praying to angels can be extremely dangerous. While God's angels can't perform outside the will of God, the fallen angels (demons) serving Satan can and often do. They're always looking for opportunities to creep into your life and create havoc.

I'm reminded of a story of a group of men who tried to cast out demons just as the apostle Paul and Jesus had done on countless occasions. Unfortunately, this group of men who sought fame through exorcism nearly lost their lives in the process. They totally missed a central truth about angels. They were ignorant and uninformed. They neglected to realize that without a personal relationship with Jesus Christ, they had no authority over evil spirits.

In Acts 19, the story is told of how these men tried to cast an evil spirit out of a man. It backfired on them. Notice the verse below:

A group of Jews was traveling from town to town casting out evil spirits. They tried to use the name of the Lord Jesus in their incantation, saying, "I command you in the name of Jesus, whom Paul preaches, to come out!" Seven sons of Sceva, a leading priest, were doing this. But one time when they tried it, the evil spirit replied, "I know Jesus, and I know Paul, but who are you?" Then the man with the evil spirit leaped on them, overpowered them, and attacked them with such violence that they fled from the house, naked and battered.   — Acts 19:13-16

Later in this book you'll understand more fully why this horrible thing happened to these men. Right now it's critically important for you to understand the biggest mistakes you can make with angels.

Mistake #1 – Never worship or pray to an angel.

While traveling several countries, I've noticed to my amazement how easy it is for good, well-meaning people to unwittingly turn their trust away from God and place it in some inanimate object. I've seen numerous angel relics in front of people's homes, or on their desks, or even hanging from their cars' rear-view mirrors. This is much like what some people do with the statue of Mary, and even others who wear a cross around their neck or carry a Saint Christopher medal in their pocket.

Is it wrong to do any of these things? No! Having them around your house or in your possession is not wrong. But when you begin thinking they might possess some kind of spiritual power or are able in some way to protect you from evil, you've made a huge mistake. It's called idolatry.

Many well-intentioned people do this. They have a belief deep down inside that the inanimate object will in some way protect them from harm. This couldn't be further from the truth.

First, when a person ignorantly or even intentionally thinks a statue of Mary or a cross around the neck or a house full of angels provides protection, they have fallen prey to one of the covert strategies of Satan. He will do what he can to get you to cast your faith onto anything else but God. Doing so is idolatry, and he knows it.

God clearly tells us in the Ten Commandments:

> You must not make for yourself an idol of any kind or an image of anything in the heavens or on the earth or in the sea. You must not bow down to them or worship them, for I, the LORD your God, am a jealous God who will not tolerate your affection for any other gods.   — Exodus 20:4-5

Idolatry happens when you exalt anything above God.

You may not be worshipping them, but allowing yourself to form some kind of belief that these objects can protect you is breaking the first of the Ten Commandments. Nothing should replace God. Not an angel. Not a Saint Christopher medal. Not even a statue of Mary.

By praying to an angel, you've elevated an angel to a place that is solely allocated to God. Putting your trust in a Saint Christopher medal for protection does the same thing. If you're filling your house with angelic knickknacks or filling your yard with statues of Mary hoping to ward off demonic spirits or evil energy, you've dangerously misplaced your trust.

Remember what God said? He is "a jealous God." There's nothing that comes close in comparison to His power and His ability to protect you. The moment you think that these other things may help you instead of God, you've started down the path that leads to idolatry.

Look at the scathing rebuke God gave to the nation of Israel in the book of Jeremiah:

> "They say to wood, 'You are my father,' and to stone, 'You gave me birth.' They have turned their backs to me and not their faces; yet when they are in trouble, they say, 'Come and save us!' Where then are the gods you made for yourselves? Let them come if they can save you when you are in trouble!"
> —Jeremiah 2:27-28

Again, am I saying that it's wrong to have angelic knickknacks throughout your house? No!

Is it wrong to have a statue of Mary in your yard or wear a cross around your neck or bury a Saint Christopher medal in your pocket? No! Absolutely not.

However, the moment you begin to place any amount of faith in those inanimate objects, you have given up some small trust in the God who loves you. If you're not trusting God 100 percent, then you're NOT trusting Him at all. Faith is an all-or-nothing virtue.

The truth is, angel figurines are nice, and they can be a nice addition to a home if you like collecting them. The only thing I'm trying to get across to you is to keep in mind that those inanimate objects have no power at all to help you. The moment you place even a small amount of trust in them, it begins an erosion of your faith in God.

Listen to the warning the apostle Paul gives about the worshipping of angels in the book of Colossians:

> Don't let anyone condemn you by insisting on pious self-denial or the worship of angels, saying they have had visions about these things. Their sinful minds have made them proud....   —Colossians 2:18

Mistake #2 – Don't ever channel an angel.

Channeling seems to have become a popular pastime today. Sadly, uninformed people have written how-to books about this subject. They know nothing of the nature of the spiritual world, and they are not only dabbling in occult activity themselves but blindly leading others to do the same. This is an incredibly dangerous thing!

I'll tell you why in just a moment, but first let me explain what channeling an angel is.

This happens when someone tries to contact an angel through the help of an individual called a "channeler" or medium. After a counselee has been placed into a trancelike state, the channeler then supposedly writes down everything the angel relays to him or her.

Channeling is nothing short of witchcraft and dabbling in the occult. While the counselee has no intention of worshipping Satan or contacting demonic forces, the sad reality is that no channeler can contact an angel of God. And since none of God's angels will allow themselves to work outside of the direct will of God, it only leaves another kind of angel that's available to send a message—a demon!

Remember, the angels of God do not work on their own volition. They strictly respond only to the call and command of God. Any attempt to channel an angel opens the opportunity for demons to work.

But can a demon provide a message to someone through a channeler? Absolutely! Demons are very knowledgeable about you, your past, and your concerns. It's very possible that the message coming from the channeler would be something only you would know about, therefore causing you to think that this truly is a message from one of God's angels.

In a moment I'm going to give you a checklist and a chart that will help you to determine what kind of angel you're dealing with. Before I do, let me first mention how Satan uses things to covertly draw you in.

The covert strategy of Satan is to appear innocent initially. He loves covering his true identity. When an unsuspected counselee begins the process of channeling angels, they have started down a dark path that can allow demons to take control. It can be the initial stages leading toward demonic possession. More about that later.

Here's where the danger lies. Demonic spirits can act on their own volition. They have been kicked out of heaven and are not under the direct command of God. Even though no demon is beyond the reach of God's eye and control, demons can and will mask their identities to appear as angels of God. When people go to channelers looking for an angel of God to speak to them, a demon spirit can easily become involved. They want to be involved.

From a demon's perspective, that plays right into their hands. If they can get you to draw your faith and focus away from God and toward anything other than God, they've done their job. Don't let this happen to you!

The Bible tells us in 1 John 4:1:

Dear friends, do not believe everyone who claims to speak by the Spirit. You must test them to see if the spirit they have comes from God. For there are many false prophets in the world.

Here are some simple facts about God's holy angels. If you are engaged with some spiritual being, please note the following:

- God's angels are NOT summoned at will.
- God's angels will NOT accept worship.
- God's angels do NOT leave us with feelings of anxiety or fear.
- God's angels do NOT leave us confused or emotionally upset.
- God's angels will NOT invite communication from you.
- God's angels will NOT offer guidance that is contrary to God or His Word.

- God's angels do NOT haunt areas. They stand in God's presence ready to serveHim.
- God's angels will point your attention, worship, and prayers only to God.

If any of the above statements are contrary to what you've experienced, you are encountering a demonic (evil) spirit.

If you feel you need help or would like to speak with someone about your experience with the spiritual world, please go to my website at:

www.AngelsUTM.com

Let us know how we can assist you! My team and I would love to help you and pray with you.

Chapter 4

Why Angels Exist

As we take a closer look at angels, you're going to quickly realize they aren't anything like the flannel-shirt wearing Michael Landon from the TV series *Highway to Heaven*, nor do they possess the same feminine beauty as Roma Downey in the TV show *Touched by an Angel*. You'll also notice they aren't anything like the bumbling character of the angel Clarence in the hit Christmas classic *It's a Wonderful Life* who's trying to earn his wings by saving George Bailey, played by actor Jimmy Stewart.

Angels are far different from how Hollywood has tried to portray them. In fact, they are far more beautiful, powerful, and fearful in design than you and I can imagine. While the Bible often portrays them as glorious, shining beings, the Bible also shows them appearing without their glorious covering, where they consequently appear as human beings. As a result, some people have mistakenly concluded that angels could be some kind of alien life form or an advanced race of human beings. They are neither.

So who are they and what are they really like?

1. Angels are created beings.

It's important for us to realize angels aren't eternally existent like God. God created them in the beginning when He made His decision to create the universe:

> Praise him, all his angels! Praise him, all the armies of heaven!
> Praise him, sun and moon! Praise him, all you twinkling stars!
> Praise him, skies above! Praise him, vapors high above the clouds!
> Let every created thing give praise to the LORD, for he issued his command, and they came into being.   —Psalm 148:2-5

As created beings, angels stand in the presence of God and continually give Him praise. They stand ready to serve His purposes. God created them for the express purpose of serving Him.

Can you imagine what it must have been like to have a front-row seat at creation? The angels were given the unique opportunity to witness God's indescribable power as He spoke all things into existence. God tells us about their enthusiastic applause at the moment of His creation. In the book of Job, God is questioning Job, and within those questions He shares with Job (and us) how the angels reacted when He spoke all things into existence:

> Where were you when I laid the earth's foundation? Tell me, if you understand. Who

marked off its dimensions? Surely you know!
Who stretched a measuring line across it?
On what were its footings set, or who laid its
cornerstone—while the morning stars sang
together and all the angels shouted for joy?
                                              —Job 38:4-7

The angels must have been overwhelmed! In
response to God's power to create the universe, all
the angels sang together and shouted with extreme
joy. I can only imagine what that must have been
like. Think about it! The sound of shouts stemming
from extreme joy from multiplied millions of angels
must have created shockwaves that penetrated
deep into space.

2. Angels are spirit beings.

If I could use one verse of the Bible to cover a lot
of ground about angels—who they are and what
their purpose is—it would be found in the book of
Hebrews. Here's what the writer of Hebrews has to
say about angels:

And of the angels He says: "Who makes His
angels spirits and His ministers a flame of
fire."   —Hebrews 1:7

Are they not all ministering spirits sent
forth to minister for thosewho will inherit
salvation?   —Hebrews 1:14

From these two verses alone, we can draw out
and understand several powerful truths about
angels.

The word "spirit" in the Bible (in its Greek form) resembles the word "breath." Like your breath, while you cannot see it, it's there. And if you've eaten any onions or garlic, everyone else knows it's there too.

God is basically telling us that angels are invisible. They are very much like the air we breathe. You can't see it, but it's there.

The Bible says that God Himself is a Spirit (John 4:24). So it makes perfect sense that God (who is a Spirit) created His angels as spirits. This means they do not possess a physical composition like human beings.

Guess who else is a spiritual being? Man! However, unlike the angels, we have a physical covering called a "body."

When God created us, remember what He said? In Genesis 1:26-27, He said: "Let us make man in Our image." Since God is a Spirit—and his angels and the rest of the heavenly host are spiritual beings—it's no wonder He created us as a spirit as well. In the book of Job, the Bible teaches:

> But there is a spirit in man, and the breath of
> the Almighty gives him understanding.
> —Job 32:8

In addition to making us spiritual beings, God did something for us He did *not* do for the angels or any other heavenly being. He gave us a physical body. Our physical bodies are confined to the physical dimension within elements of time and space.

God also gave us a soul, the seat of our emotions and intellect. So, like God, you're a tripartite being. You are made up of three parts—a body, soul, and spirit. I like to put it this way, "You are a spiritual being who has a soul that's temporarily enshrouded with a body."

The apostle Paul also put it this way in the first book of Thessalonians:

> Now may the God of peace make you holy in every way, and may your whole spirit and soul and body be kept blameless until our Lord Jesus Christ comes again.
> —1 Thessalonians 5:23

Someone once asked me, "Are angels the same as ghosts?"

It's a good question, especially since the Holy Spirit is referred to as the Holy Ghost in some old biblical translations. However, ghosts are often thought of as human beings who are deceased and roaming the earth with unfinished business. That's not what angels are. They are not an advanced form of the human race. They are not aliens. Nor are they even deceased human beings roaming the earth waiting to enter into the light. They were created as spirit beings with the express purpose of serving God.

3. Angels are ministering spirits.

Using both verses above from the book of Hebrews, angels are also a special kind of spirit. The verse above says they are "ministers" or "ministering spirits."

Another translation puts it this way: they are "servants." In fact, this is exactly how an angel describes himself to John, one of Jesus's disciples.

Notice what the angel says of himself in the scripture below:

> And the angel said to me, "Write this: Blessed are those who are invited to the wedding feast of the Lamb." And he added, "These are true words that come from God." Then I fell down at his feet to worship him, but he said, "No, don't worship me. I am a servant of God, just like you and your brothers and sisters who testify about their faith in Jesus. Worship only God." — Revelation 22:8-9

4. Angels are sent spirits.

In the verse above (Hebrews 1:14), did you notice what else angels are? They are ministering spirits who are "sent forth." In other words, the angels of God are sent beings. They do not act on their own volition. They respond only to God's commands.

While many people would like to believe God's angels can be prayed to and act on their own volition, they don't want to do that. That would be an act of rebellion. It would defeat the purpose for which they were created. Therefore, from this verse we can see that there is someone who commands these angels and sends them forth. Who is it?

It's God! God sends them. Throughout the Scriptures, we see God as the One who does the sending forth of angels. Note the verses below:

> And God sent an angel to Jerusalem to destroy it. — 1 Chronicles 21:15

Then the Lord sent an angel who cut down every mighty man of valor, leader and captain in the camp of the king of Assyria.
— 2 Chronicles 32:21

My God sent His angel and shut the lions' mouths, so that they have not hurt me, because I was found innocent before Him.
— Daniel 6:22

Now in the sixth month the angel Gabriel was sent by God to a city of Galilee named Nazareth.   — Luke 1:26

And the Lord God of the holy prophets sent His angel to show His servants the things which must shortly take place.
— Revelation 22:6

Angels have seen what God can do when rebellion takes place. They know and fully understand the consequences of Satan's rebellion and those that followed him. They've also witnessed the creation of the Lake of Fire for Satan and his angels. As a result, God's angels seek only to serve Him and be sent at His command.

Praise the Lord, you angels, you mighty ones who carry out his plans, listening for each of his commands.   — Psalm 103:20

Their job is not to answer our call. It's to answer God's call. They don't listen to us. They listen to God. Angels will only carry out God's wishes, and they will only do so at His command.

5. Angels are messengers from God.

Both the Hebrew and Greek word used for angel means "messenger." The Hebrew word *malak* is used in the Old Testament 233 times, and the Greek word *angelos* is used 176 times in the New Testament. Each time, it simply means "messenger." As ministering spirits, angels bring messages to believers or those who "will inherit salvation."

Notice in the verses below how an angel delivered a message to both Peter and Philip, both believers in Jesus Christ:

> Suddenly, there was a bright light in the cell, and an angel of the Lord stood before Peter. The angel struck him on the side to awaken him and said, "Quick! Get up!" And the chains fell off his wrists. Then the angel told him, "Get dressed and put on your sandals." And he did. "Now put on your coat and follow me," the angel ordered. So Peter left the cell, following the angel. — Acts 12:7-9

> As for Philip, an angel of the Lord said to him, "Go south down the desert road that runs from Jerusalem to Gaza." — Acts 8:26

Now, notice in the following verse how God sent an angel to an unbeliever by the name of Cornelius. However, keep in mind that the angel's purpose was to lead this man into a relationship with Jesus Christ!

> One afternoon about three o'clock, he had a vision in which he saw an angel of God

coming toward him. "Cornelius!" the angel said. Cornelius stared at him in terror. "What is it, sir?" he asked the angel. And the angel replied, "Your prayers and gifts to the poor have been received by God as an offering! Now send some men to Joppa, and summon a man named Simon Peter. He is staying with Simon, a tanner who lives near the seashore." As soon as the angel was gone, Cornelius called two of his household servants and a devout soldier, one of his personal attendants. He told them what had happened and sent them off to Joppa.

— Acts 10:3-8

One of the most incredible stories of the Old Testament is about an angel's attempt to bring a message from God to Daniel. It took this angel exactly twenty-one days to do it. Although the angel received the message on the very first day of Daniel's prayer, this angel was held up from delivering that message.

For twenty-one days the angel was blocked by the Prince of Persia, which was either Satan himself or one of his most powerful high-ranking demons. It wasn't until Michael the archangel arrived to fight against these evil forces that the angel could then get through to Daniel here on earth. Notice this amazing story below, and keep in mind that Daniel had been praying for three weeks, or twenty-one days:

So I was left there all alone to see this amazing vision. My strength left me, my face grew deathly pale, and I felt very weak.

Then I heard the man speak, and when I heard the sound of his voice, I fainted and lay there with my face to the ground. Just then a hand touched me and lifted me, still trembling, to my hands and knees. And the man said to me, "Daniel, you are very precious to God, so listen carefully to what I have to say to you. Stand up, for I have been sent to you." When he said this to me, I stood up, still trembling. Then he said, "Don't be afraid, Daniel. Since the first day you began to pray for understanding and to humble yourself before your God, your request has been heard in heaven. I have come in answer to your prayer. But for twenty-one days the spirit prince of the kingdom of Persia blocked my way. Then Michael, one of the archangels, came to help me, and I left him there with the spirit prince of the kingdom of Persia. Now I am here to explain what will happen to your people in the future, for this vision concerns a time yet to come.   —Daniel 10:8,9, 12-14

In the New Testament, we see an angel delivering a message to the women who came to the tomb of Christ after He had risen from the grave:

There was a violent earthquake, for an angel of the Lord came down from heaven and, going to the tomb, rolled back the stone and sat on it. His appearance was like lightning, and his clothes were white as snow. The guards were so afraid of him that they shook and became like dead men. The angel said to the women, "Do not be afraid, for I know that you are looking for Jesus, who was crucified. He is not here; he has risen, just as he said. Come and see the place where he lay. Then go quickly and tell his disciples: 'He has risen from the dead and is going ahead of you into Galilee. There you will see him.' Now I have told you.

—Matthew 28:2-7

We could go on with several messages that angels gave to Mary, to Joseph, to the shepherds at the birth of Christ, and to John. Suffice it to say, angels are also God's messengers.

6. Angels minister only to believers.

Okay, here's where some people might get really upset! This verse not only teaches us they are ministering spirits sent from God, but it also tells us what kind of individuals they serve.

Angels serve only those who have or will receive Jesus Christ as their Savior.

While God's mission is to help all men whether they be for God or against Him, God loves all men! But when it comes to the ministry of angels, God has restricted their ministry capacity. God will only allow them to act upon His command. And He'll only allow them to minister to believers in Jesus Christ and those "who will be heirs of salvation."

Remember what God says in the book of Hebrews:

Are they not all ministering spirits sent
forth to minister for those who will inherit
salvation?   —Hebrews 1:14

You will never find an angel of God in the Bible
sent to help an unbeliever. I don't know why, but
this is the way God has designed it to be. God has
designed angels specifically to be sent to minister
only to those who are followers of Jesus Christ.

In fact, it's interesting to note that Jesus told
His audience one day that those who accept Him
as Savior are announced before the angels of God.
Conversely, those who deny Him as Savior are
denied before the angels of God.

Look at what Jesus said:

I tell you the truth, everyone who acknowl-
edges me publicly here on earth, the Son of
Man will also acknowledge in the presence
of God's angels. But anyone who denies me
here on earth will be denied before God's
angels.   —Luke 12:8-9

Does this mean Jesus and the angels don't care
about unbelievers? No, they do care. They care very
deeply. In fact, Jesus cared so much for unbelievers
that He left heaven, took on the physical form of a
man, placed man's sins upon Himself, submitted
Himself to the cruelty of the Roman army, allowed
Himself to be savagely sacrificed on a cross, held
back from asking angels to rescue Him, and three
days later rose again from the grave to make it
possible for all unbelievers to enjoy eternity with
God in heaven. There's no greater love than this!

As far as the angels and their concern for unbelievers, they care, but their caring is really irrelevant. Why? Because they can't do anything about it. Angels cannot and will not exceed the bounds God has placed upon them. Angels seek only to please God, not man.

However, this shouldn't upset anyone. The idea of not having an angel protecting you is nothing to worry about. Your greatest concern should not be whether you have a guardian angel or not. It should be about gaining God's protection and seeking His guidance.

God loves you and wants you to give your life to Him. He wants to protect you and is working in your life to bring you to His Son, Jesus Christ. But the choice is yours.

Angels may be able to do things we humans can't, but they aren't God. God is the One who cares about us the most. We are the focus of His attention. We are the apple of His eye. The Bible is replete with scriptures and stories where God loves the unbeliever, helps the unbeliever, elevates the unbeliever to great status for reasons only He knows. God can protect an unbeliever at any time. It's just that His angels don't serve that purpose.

To worry about the angels not guarding someone is a concern that's misplaced. Angels can't do what God can do!

Regardless of what you and I think or how we feel about it, God has restricted the angels that serve Him to ministering solely to those who have given their lives to Him. To help an unbeliever would be in direct conflict with their primary purpose — to serve and worship God and to obey His commands explicitly:

Praise the Lord, you angels, you mighty ones
who carry out his plans, listening for each of
his commands.   —Psalm 103:20

While the angels of God are restricted in whom they serve, the fallen angels or demons aren't. They are not under the direct authority of God. While they are powerless before God and not able to do anything without His knowing, they follow Satan's command. They've been kicked out of heaven and placed under Satan's limited authority.

The scary thing is that they often can and will respond to any request you might make to them. They can appear as angels of God. They enjoy this deception. They will do anything they can to enter into your life and take control—and most importantly distract your attention and faith away from God.

Here's why. Satan's desire has always been to be like God or to counterfeit God. If the demons can convince you they are angels of God and the message they bring is from God, they are doing their job. Any opportunity they have to divert your attention away from God, they will take it. Drawing you away from God is their primary purpose.

The stunning reality of the spiritual world is this. If you're not a believer in Jesus Christ, Satan can hold you captive at his will. Look at what the apostle Paul said about this dangerous phenomenon:

Then they will come to their senses and
escape from the devil's trap. For they have
been held captive by him to do whatever he
wants.   —2 Timothy 2:26

I think that's exactly what happened with men like Josef Stalin and Adolf Hitler. They dabbled in the occult and Satan took advantage of them. Demonic forces used them like pawns on a chessboard to commit horrible acts against humanity, especially God's people, the Jews.

That's why dabbling in the occult or even praying to angels can be dangerous. Satan's power to influence people is real. Don't go looking for him. He knows exactly where you are. He's looking for opportunities to kill, steal, and destroy your life, your marriage, your children, and everything you hold dear.

Jesus offers this warning about Satan's purpose:

> The thief's purpose is to steal and kill and destroy. My purpose is to give them a rich and satisfying life.   —John 19:10

While Satan's desire and purpose is to seize the joy and happiness God intended for you to have, Jesus' purpose and desire is for you to find it. That's why it's so important for you to give your life to Christ.

Chapter 5

What Angels Look Like

When the pastor of our church asked me to share my study on angels, many people were excited. Many of them had never heard a teaching on angels. In fact, Billy Graham once said, "Despite having read literally thousands of personal accounts of people seeing these amazing beings, I've never heard a sermon on angels."

So I was a bit surprised when one of my biggest fans, a wonderful and godly woman, approached me with concern written across her face. She told me, "Randy, I'm so sorry. I just can't come to your study on angels."

Before I could say anything, she continued, "You know I enjoy hearing you every time you speak, but if you're not going to preach on Jesus, I'm just not interested."

I smiled at her and reassured her that it was okay. I told her, "I just want you to know, I'm not teaching about angels because I want to glorify them or exalt them. God wouldn't want me doing that, nor would the angels. In fact, I'm teaching people about angels because God has taught us about angels in His Word. What God reveals in His Word about angels opens up a greater understanding of Himself, His love, His power, His glory, His work, His grace, and the wonderful and exciting plan He has for you and me."

In this chapter, I'd like to share with you what God's angels really look like.

1. Angels are absolutely stunning in beauty.

John, the writer of Revelation, recorded the angel he saw as having a bright splendor about him that illuminated the earth.

> After all this I saw another angel come down from heaven with great authority, and the earth grew bright with his splendor.
> —Revelation 18:1

Daniel was given the opportunity to actually see the angel Gabriel in his full glory. What you're about to read is a riveting account of Daniel's encounter with this powerful archangel. The story reveals probably more than you'd like to know. But before we go too deep, let's take a brief look at how Daniel described the archangel:

> On April 23, as I was standing on the bank of the great Tigris River, I looked up and saw a man dressed in linen clothing, with a belt of pure gold around his waist. His body looked like a precious gem. His face flashed like lightning, and his eyes flamed like torches. His arms and feet shone like

polished bronze, and his voice roared like a
vast multitude of people.   — Daniel 10:4-6

As terror flowed through Daniel's veins, he
recorded the image of Gabriel as best he could.
Notice the words Daniel used to describe him. His
body had a beautiful bluish color like topaz. His
face was so bright that the only word Daniel could
think of to describe his brilliance was "lightning."

Then he noted how he fearfully looked into
Gabriel's eyes as they appeared as flames of fire.
Daniel described them as "torches." His arms and
legs looked like shining brass, and he had a voice
that resonated a blast equal to that of thunder.

Many times, as I've read this verse, I've thought
of the challenges that Steven Spielberg and other
Hollywood directors would face in utilizing the
latest in film technology to recreate the beauty of
Gabriel. However, just like a picture of the majestic
Rockies of Colorado, there's nothing like seeing it
in person!

Daniel had never seen anything like this before.
Nothing on earth could prepare him for what he
saw that day. Listen to how he described his reaction to the sight of Gabriel's appearing. This is
typical of people in the Bible who were given the
chance to see an angel in his full glory:

> Only I, Daniel, saw this vision. The men with
> me saw nothing, but they were suddenly
> terrified and ran away to hide. So I was left
> there all alone to see this amazing vision. My
> strength left me, my face grew deathly pale,
> and I felt very weak. Then I heard the man

speak, and when I heard the sound of his
voice, I fainted and lay there with my face to
the ground.   — Daniel 10:7-8

Daniel was gripped with uncontrollable fear. In
fact, his friends — who didn't see Gabriel — were so
utterly frightened they ran away.

Have you had anything scare you so much that
you wanted to hide? Or have you had anything
scare you so much you literally passed out?

That's exactly what happened to Daniel. As
Gabriel began to speak, he said he went into "a
deep sleep." Actually, he passed out with his face
falling forward to the ground. Only after the touch
of Gabriel's hand was Daniel able to crawl up on
his knees trembling in fear.

Daniel's opportunity to see the glory of an angel
is only one of many accounts throughout the Bible
that describe the same reaction.

Look at what happened to some elite soldiers of
the Roman army who were given orders to guard
the tomb of Jesus:

For an angel of the Lord came down from
heaven, rolled aside the stone, and sat on
it. His face shone like lightning, and his
clothing was as white as snow. The guards
shook with fear when they saw him, and
they fell into a dead faint. — Matthew 28:2-4

These men of battle had never seen such a thing,
nor had they felt such fear.

In another case, John, one of Jesus's disciples,
was exiled on the isle of Patmos for preaching the
gospel. During that imprisonment, God unveiled

a revelation of future events that foretold the end of the world. He recorded those events in the book of Revelation. During that time, he had encounters with several mighty angels. In Revelation 10:1, he describes the angel this way:

> Then I saw another mighty angel coming down from heaven, surrounded by a cloud, with a rainbow over his head. His face shone like the sun, and his feet were like pillars of fire.

We could go on with more stories, but that should suffice to show you just how incredibly beautiful angels are as they bask in the glorious presence of almighty God. Just think, one day we will bask in the Lord's presence and radiate His glory just like the angels!

2. Angels are powerful beings.

> Bless the Lord, you His angels, who excel in strength, who do His word. —Psalm 103:20

Angels are often referred to as "mighty" in Scripture. In 2 Thessalonians, the apostle Paul speaks of a future day when God will take vengeance on mankind for refusing to obey Him and will bring His mighty angels with Him:

> And God will provide rest for you who are being persecuted and also for us when the Lord Jesus appears from heaven. He will come with his mighty angels, in flaming fire, bringing judgment on those who don't

91

know God and on those who refuse to obey the Good News of our Lord Jesus.

— 2 Thessalonians 1:7

John records the strength of a mighty angel when describing an event in Revelation:

Then a mighty angel picked up a boulder the size of a huge millstone. He threw it into the ocean and shouted, "Just like this, the great city Babylon will be thrown down with violence and will never be found again."

— Revelation 18:21

As mentioned before, angels are mighty in strength when compared to man's strength. However, they have no strength when compared to the power and strength of almighty God.

For those who try to put angels on a pedestal, it's important to know that angels are:

- not all-powerful
- not everywhere-present
- not all-knowing

They are not anything like God!

In fact, Jesus even admits that their knowledge is very limited. When His disciples asked Him about the end of the world, Jesus said that even the angels didn't know when that time would be — only God knew.

However, no one knows the day or hour when these things will happen, not even the angels in heaven . . . Only the Father knows.
— Matthew 24:36

3. Angels have great mobility.

One of the most fascinating studies on angels is found in the book of Daniel. There you'll see just how swiftly they can move, with the power to go from one realm to the other:

I went on praying and confessing my sin and the sin of my people, pleading with the LORD my God for Jerusalem, his holy mountain. As I was praying, Gabriel, whom I had seen in the earlier vision, came swiftly to me at the time of the evening sacrifice. He explained to me, "Daniel, I have come here to give you insight and understanding. The moment you began praying, a command was given. And now I am here to tell you what it was, for you are very precious to God. Listen carefully so that you can understand the meaning of your vision."
— Daniel 9:20-23

I want you to notice a couple of things.

First, see how swiftly the archangel Gabriel responds to Daniel. He tells Daniel, "The moment you began praying, a command was given."

The very moment Daniel started praying to God, God issued a command to Gabriel to send Daniel a message. Daniel records how swiftly all this happened. He said, "As I was praying, Gabriel, whom I had seen in the earlier vision, came swiftly to me at the time of the evening sacrifice." Before Daniel had finished praying, the archangel Gabriel was dispatched from God in answer to Daniel's prayer. Now that's fast!

Secondly, Gabriel goes from the presence of God in heaven and from the spiritual realm directly into Daniel's presence on earth in the physical realm. Angels can easily transport themselves in and out of the spiritual and physical realms. You can see this in other occasions throughout the Bible.

In Genesis 28, the Bible records how Jacob witnessed in a dream angels going from one realm to the other:

> And he dreamed, and behold a ladder set up on the earth, and the top of it reached to heaven: and behold the angels of God ascending and descending on it.
> —Genesis 28:12

However, the reality of this is more than just a dream. Jesus told one of His disciples, Nathanael, that one day he would see the heavens open up and witness the angels going from one realm to another.

> And he saith unto him, Verily, verily, I say unto you, Hereafter ye shall see heaven open, and the angels of God ascending and descending upon the Son of man.
> —John 1:51

4. Angels are in great quantity.

No scripture gives us the exact number of angels God created, but we do know their number is practically incalculable.

John tried to give us some idea of what he saw in heaven in the book of Revelation:

> Then I looked, and I heard the voice of many angels around the throne, the living creatures, and the elders; and the number of them was ten thousand times ten thousand, and thousands of thousands.
>
> —Revelation 5:11

One mathematician calculated this number to be about 100,000 million. However, John was only giving us his account of a nearly indescribable amount of angels he saw worshipping God in heaven.

Another verse in Hebrews puts it this way:

> But you have come to Mount Zion and to the city of the living God, the heavenly Jerusalem, to an innumerable company of angels.   —Hebrews 12:22

Only God knows the number of angels He created. While it would be interesting to know, it doesn't really matter. God knew exactly how many He was willing to create and use.

5. Angels are intelligent beings.

While angels are limited on what they know, they do know a lot more than we do. Angels are very in tune with what's going on in the world. Notice the verse below:

> To bring about this change of affairs your servant Joab has done this thing; but my lord is wise, according to the wisdom of the angel of God, to know everything that is in the earth.   — 2 Samuel 14:20

6. Angels are emotional beings.

Angels can express emotions. Notice what Jesus said in Luke 15:

> In the same way, there is joy in the presence of God's angels when even one sinner repents.   — Luke 15:10

In fact, I find it fascinating how much the angel Gabriel is impressed with God's love for Daniel. At least three times Gabriel mentions how important Daniel is to God:

> As I was praying, Gabriel, whom I had seen in the earlier vision, came swiftly to me at the time of the evening sacrifice. He explained to me, "Daniel, I have come here to give you insight and understanding. The moment you began praying, a command was given. And now I am here to tell you what it was, for you are very precious to God. Listen carefully so that you can understand the meaning of your vision."   — Daniel 9:21-23

And the man said to me, "Daniel, you are very precious to God, so listen carefully to what I have to say to you." — Daniel 10:11

Then the one who looked like a man touched me again, and I felt my strength returning. "Don't be afraid," he said, "for you are very precious to God. Peace! Be encouraged! Be strong!" — Daniel 10:18-19

The angels marvel at God's love for us. They know we are the apple of His eye. They are absolutely fascinated with the concept that the magnificent, holy, and all-powerful God in whose presence they stand and worship every day would love such a sinful creature as man. When you think about it, it is amazing!

The more unique qualities of angels:

1. Angels never appear with wings.

I find it fascinating that in every instance an angel appears, they appear as men *without* wings. In fact, that's exactly how they're described by Daniel:

On April 23rd, as I was standing on the bank of the great Tigris River, I looked up and saw a man dressed in linen clothing, with a belt of pure gold around his waist. His body looked like a precious gem. His face flashed like lightning, and his eyes flamed like torches. His arms and feet shone like polished bronze, and his voice roared like a vast multitude of people. — Daniel 10:4-6

Interesting point: The Bible never once speaks of angels as having wings!

I know this may come as a shock to many people, but nowhere in the Bible does God speak of angels as having wings. They may have wings, but God does not tell us they do.

In contrast, God provides us a lot of information about the wings of the cherubim, the wings of the seraphim, as well as the unique wings of the four living beings. He goes into great detail about their wings. However, in all of the scriptures where men describe the angels they see, not one of them mentions wings. We know John saw many angels in the Revelation. Although he describes in great detail how angels look, he never mentions anything about their wings.

Is it because they don't have wings?

I don't know. God never discusses that issue. Many good people say they have personally seen angels. I don't doubt that many of them have. Some of these people I know personally. And while not all of them have seen angels with wings, some actually say they have. For some good reason, God doesn't discuss it in His Word. That is a topic we may have to delay until we're in heaven to know for sure.

2. Angels can appear in physical form.

Angels have a wide and varied responsibility. Some of those responsibilities include protecting us—Peter, for example, in the book of Acts.

Do you remember what an angel did for Peter one day while he was imprisoned for preaching the good news about Jesus? The legal authorities had thrown him into a dungeon to prevent him from sharing more about the resurrection of Jesus. While in a dungeon, Peter prayed for God's direction and help, much like we do today. What happened next took everyone by surprise, even Peter!

> But during the night an angel of the Lord opened the doors of the jail and brought them out.   — Acts 5:19

Imagine this if you can. Peter is securely locked up in a dark, dank Roman jail for preaching about Jesus. Then suddenly the doors open, and he's led out by an angel through several sets of doors and eventually to freedom.

Try explaining that to the authorities!

I can only imagine what Peter, a simple fisherman, might have said in his defense as he tried to explain his unusual and untimely release: "Well, you know, I was just sitting there thinking about how I really hated this dungeon when all of a sudden this guy with glowing clothes appeared. Yeah, I was freaked out as well as everybody else with me! Then the doors just kind of flung open. It's true! Ask anyone who was with me. Anyway, after the doors swung open, this glowing guy waved his hand to follow him. My friends and I just looked at each other and thought, hey, why not? So we walked out. As we followed him, door after door just kept opening up right in front of us. I'm sure you would have done the same thing, right?"

The religious and legal authorities got confirmation from the guards and realized something supernatural must have taken place, so they let them go. Can you imagine what an incredible experience that must have been for Peter and those others with him?

In fact, when thinking about how angels interact with us, I am reminded of this most fascinating verse in the book of Hebrews. In it, God warns:

> Don't forget to show hospitality to strangers, for some who have done this have entertained angels without realizing it!
> —Hebrews 13:2

In this one verse, God elevates our interaction with angels to a whole new level. They're not only invisible beings working behind the scenes; there may be times when God allows them, disguised as other people, to interact with us.

You first see angels appearing in human form in Genesis 18. On this occasion, the Lord told Abraham about the upcoming destruction of Sodom and Gomorrah. On that mission, God brought two angels to go before Him into the town of Sodom. Their job was not only to warn Abraham's nephew (Lot) about the impending doom, but to help him escape the city before it happened.

While approaching his tent, Abraham looked up and described them as "three men standing nearby."

> One day Abraham was sitting at the entrance to his tent during the hottest part of the day. He looked up and noticed three men standing nearby. When he saw them, he ran to meet them and welcomed them, bowing low to the ground. —Genesis 18:1-2

Notice how the Lord allows the angels to appear in human form here. In fact, these angels not only ate the food offered by Abraham, but they also went into the town of Sodom. Lot saw them as mere human beings.

> That evening the two angels came to the entrance of the city of Sodom. Lot was sitting there, and when he saw them, he stood up to meet them. Then he welcomed them and bowed with his face to the ground. "My lords," he said, "come to my home to wash your feet, and be my guests for the night. You may then get up early in the morning and be on your way again."
> —Genesis 19:1-2

A few verses later, we see how the townspeople call them "men."

> But before they retired for the night, all the men of Sodom, young and old, came from all over the city and surrounded the house. They shouted to Lot, "Where are the men who came to spend the night with you? Bring them out to us so we can have sex with them!"
> —Genesis 19:4-5

Again, that fascinating verse from Hebrews 13:2—"Don't forget to show hospitality to strangers, for some who have done this have entertained angels without realizing it!" —is why I think it's so important how we treat other people. I've often responded to complete strangers with love and respect, sometimes even offering money if they appear needy or homeless on the streets. I always wonder, "Is this a test from God? Could this be an angel? Does God want to see how I respond to a complete stranger?"

I'm not telling you to start handing out $100 bills to complete strangers or to fill the hand of every needy person on the street. However, I have given a $100 bill to a complete stranger, but I use wisdom when I do. I'll usually spend some time with them to better understand their need.

I've also offered money to the needy on the streets in many major cities across the country. But first I try to discern whether this is a test from God. I spend a few moments with them and talk to them about Jesus. I always want to know before I give them any money if they know Jesus as their personal Savior. Some say yes. Others say no. Either way, I'm always asking myself, "God, what do You want me to do?"

That's why the Bible teaches us to test the spirits.

> Beloved, do not believe every spirit, but test the spirits, whether they are of God; because many false prophets have gone out into the world. By this you know the Spirit of God: Every spirit that confesses that Jesus Christ has come in the flesh is of God, and every spirit that does not confess that Jesus Christ has come in the flesh is not of God.
> —1 John 4:1-3

3. Angels are always seen as men.

If you look in the book of Daniel, Daniel describes the angel Gabriel as a man.

Then it happened, when I, Daniel, had seen
the vision and was seeking the meaning, that
suddenly there stood before me one having
the appearance of a man. — Daniel 8:15

Just before God destroyed the wicked city of
Sodom, the men of the city tried to have sex with
the angels sent to rescue Lot, and they saw them
as men:

They shouted to Lot, "Where are the men
who came to spend the night with you?
Bring them out to us so we can have sex with
them!" — Genesis 19:5

All angels in the Bible appear as men or have
the masculine pronoun "he" or "him" attached to
them. Never once do you see a female angel or an
angel referred to with feminine pronouns.

Unlike the physical world where man was
given the command to populate the world beginning with only two beings, Adam and Eve, the
spiritual world is quite different. God created
them with no need to populate. God spoke and
the number of angels, the kinds of angels, and
the various kinds of other spiritual beings were
simply formed. They remain at a constant number
so there's no need to populate.

This is one of the reasons why Jesus scolded
the religious leaders of His day when they tried to
test Him with a question about marriage. Listen to
what He said:

For when the dead rise, they will neither
marry nor be given in marriage. In this
respect they will be like the angels in heaven.
— Matthew 22:30

There's been a lot of confusion about this verse
so let me explain what Jesus was actually trying
to imply. Jesus is not saying your spouse and you
aren't going to know each other in heaven. He's not
implying anything other than this: marriage is not
needed in heaven. The angels don't need to populate so there's no need to be given in marriage. I have
no doubt you'll know your spouse and family —
and have the opportunity to be with them — in
heaven. There are way too many personal testimo-
nies of people who have died and returned to their
bodies. In fact, Jesus tells us a story in Luke 16 that
this is so:

There was a certain rich man who was
clothed in purple and fine linen and fared
sumptuously every day. But there was a
certain beggar named Lazarus, full of sores,
who was laid at his gate, desiring to be fed
with the crumbs which fell from the rich
man's table. Moreover, the dogs came and
licked his sores. So it was that the beggar
died, and was carried by the angels to
Abraham's bosom. The rich man also died
and was buried. And being in torments
in Hades, he lifted up his eyes and saw
Abraham afar off, and Lazarus in his bosom.
Then he cried and said, "Father Abraham,
have mercy on me, and send Lazarus that

13

he may dip the tip of his finger in water and cool my tongue; for I am tormented in this flame." —Luke 16:19-24

What I'm trying to show you is this: Jesus tells us a story of two people—a rich man and Lazarus—who died and saw different outcomes. One went into God's presence, the other to hell. Notice, however, they saw each other and knew each other. The rich man had lived well past the days of Abraham, but for some reason he knew him in the afterlife.

If you draw any other interpretation from this, you're simply misunderstanding the context of Jesus's message.

4. Angels know future events only as God reveals to them.

Notice how an angel informs Daniel of future events:

I have been standing beside Michael to support and strengthen him since the first year of the reign of Darius the Mede. Now then, I will reveal the truth to you. Three more Persian kings will reign, to be succeeded by a fourth, far richer than the others. He will use his wealth to stir up everyone to fight against the kingdom of Greece. Then a mighty king will rise to power who will rule with great authority and accomplish everything he sets out to do. But at the height of his power, his kingdom will be broken apart and divided into four parts. It will not be ruled by the king's descendants, nor will the kingdom hold the authority it once had. For his empire will be uprooted and given to others. The king of the south will increase in power, but one of his own officials will become more powerful than he and will rule his kingdom with great strength.

—Daniel 11:1-5

Angels aren't privy to all future events, only to those God allows them to know. God is the One who reigns over all future events, not the angels. He reveals those plans only as a necessary item. In fact, not all angels know as much as other angels. That may seem strange, but each angel has his own responsibility and each angel is given from God what information is necessary for that angel.

Notice how Daniel describes the event below. He's speaking directly to the archangel Gabriel. Gabriel is presenting to Daniel the events that would shape the end times. As he does, a couple of other angels listen to Gabriel's message, and one of them is very inquisitive about how long these events will last. From this passage below, it seems that some angels know more specifically about future events than others:

Then I heard two holy ones talking to each other. One of them asked, "How long will the events of this vision last? How long will the rebellion that causes desecration stop the daily sacrifices? How long will the Temple and heaven's army be trampled on?" The other replied, "It will take 2,300 evenings

and mornings; then the Temple will be made
right again." —Daniel 8:13-14

We've already covered a lot of ground regarding
angels—why they exist, what they look like, why
you should know about them—and next we'll turn
our attention to a question that may be at the fore-
front of your mind. Keep reading!

Chapter 6

What Angels Are Doing Right Now

In 1973 I made the biggest decision of my life. It changed the course of my thinking, my ambitions, and my life. It set me on a path to do something I never dreamed of doing. The setting was the Circle C Ranch in Edgerton, Kansas, and the speaker that stormy night was John Ankerberg. In between bursts of thunder, he challenged us teenagers to start sharing our faith in Jesus Christ. It was an incredibly moving message, and I was profoundly touched.

Dr. Al Metsker, the founder of Kansas City Youth for Christ (now called YouthFront), approached the stage. He invited any young man who felt led to share his faith and not be ashamed to do so. Anyone who did so could join his preaching club for boys. He looked around the room and asked us to stand up if we wanted to join. Somebody behind me kicked me in the backside and told me to stand up. So I did. I joined the club and began a path for which I could never thank God enough. That kick in the behind was exactly what I needed!

I learned how to preach at Al's Preacher Boys Club. Soon I started speaking to Bible clubs and youth events throughout the Midwest. I was a shy kid and never once envisioned myself speaking in front of a group of people. However, here I was practically doing a speaking tour just as I was turning sixteen.

God moved so mightily in those youth meetings. Scores of kids received Christ and many others recommitted their lives to Christ. In fact, so many kids were responding for prayer at the end of each twenty-minute message that I actually thought I was doing something wrong. Kids were so deeply moved by the Spirit of God they were crying all over the place. I wasn't used to this stuff!

During my sophomore year of high school, I spoke so many times that during the beginning of football season as a junior at Grandview High School, I chose to give up football, my greatest love, so I could preach the gospel of Christ.

I shared my decision to leave football with our head football coach, Coach Tavenaro. He didn't take that very well. The timing was very unfortunate too. He had just told me he was considering starting me as one of the team's running backs. That was when I dropped the bomb.

During the next couple of years, my speaking opportunities became more frequent. God was doing some amazing things. By the time I graduated high school, my calendar showed more than one hundred speaking engagements where I had presented my one and only message: "The Biological Death of Jesus Christ."

After a year at the University of Missouri in Kansas City, while still considering a medical career, I received a phone call from Dr. Al Metsker. Dr. Al, as he was so affectionately called, invited me to join the team of evangelists he was forming at Youth for Christ. He wanted me to pray about the possibility of dropping my goal to become a medical doctor and join him in reaching teenagers all over the country with the gospel. He also invited me to help him with his radio and television programs. Obviously, for a kid who had just turned nineteen, it was an offer too good to pass up. So I said yes.

In an effort to be the best evangelist I could be, I listened carefully to the great evangelists of the late 1970s such as Billy Graham, James Robison, Manley Beasley, and John R. Rice. I read everything they presented. I probably lifted more material from John R. Rice's *Sword of the Lord* newspaper than just about anybody. Well, if truth be told, I'm sure a lot of preachers were guilty of doing the same thing. They presented some phenomenal messages, and it was hard not to "glean" a thought or two.

As Rick Warren of Saddleback Church once jokingly said while speaking to several hundred pastors, "The first time you share a thought from a good sermon, you generally quote the person. The second time you share it, you tend to say, 'I've heard it said.' Then, the third time you share it, you start saying, 'I've always said.'" Hundreds of pastors laughed because it's true!

However, there is one thing I've quoted a lot, and I give John R. Rice all the credit. Before he died in 1980, I received a rare opportunity to meet Dr. Rice, speak with him, and hear him preach. During a message at one of his meetings, he made a comment I could never get out of my mind. He said something to this effect: "If our eyes could take a glimpse of what's going on in the spiritual world, we would be absolutely amazed! We'd see angels and demons fighting all around us — fighting over our lives, fighting over our marriages, and fighting over control of our children."

That thought stunned me. I've never forgotten it. Most importantly, what Dr. Rice said was biblically true. I shared this story because it has direct bearing on the topic of this chapter.

Let's turn our attention to what angels are actually doing right now.

What Are Angels Doing in Heaven?

Angels, as we've learned, are servant spirits. They serve both God and man. However, their sole focus isn't serving man, it's serving God. Angels are just as fearful and amazed at God as we are. Unlike us, they have the distinct privilege of seeing Him in all His majesty and glory. They stand before His presence each day. They receive messages from His holy lips. And they worship Him continuously as a natural byproduct of who He is.

You alone are the Lord. You made the skies and the heavens and all the stars. You made the earth and the seas and everything in them. You preserve them all, and the angels of heaven worship you.   —Nehemiah 9:6

Look at how they worship God. We should be doing the same thing!

1. They are worshipping God continuously.

Notice how all the heavenly host worships God both day and night:

Each of these living beings had six wings, and their wings were covered all over with eyes, inside and out. Day after day and night after night they keep on saying, "Holy, holy, holy is the Lord God, the Almighty — the one who always was, who is, and who is still to come. Then I looked, and I heard the voice of many angels around the throne, the living creatures, and the elders; and the number of them was ten thousand times ten thousand, and thousands of thousands, saying with a loud voice: "Worthy is the Lamb who was slain; to receive power and riches and wisdom, and strength and honor and glory and blessing!"   — Revelation 5:11-12

2. They are worshipping God enthusiastically.

Look at how loud the worship is! Just the worship from the seraphim is so loud it shakes the foundations of God's throne.

I saw the Lord. He was sitting on a lofty throne, and the train of his robe filled the Temple. Attending him were mighty seraphim, each having six wings. With two wings they covered their faces, with two they covered their feet, and with two they flew. They were calling out to each other,

"Holy, holy, holy is the Lord of Heaven's Armies! The whole earth is filled with his glory!" Their voices shook the Temple to its foundations, and the entire building was filled with smoke.   —Isaiah 6:1-2

3. They are worshipping God in humility.

Notice the humility we see with the host in heaven:

> Whenever the living beings give glory and honor and thanks to the one sitting on the throne (the one who lives forever and ever), the twenty-four elders fall down and worship the one sitting on the throne (the one who lives forever and ever). And they lay their crowns before the throne and say, "You are worthy, O Lord our God, to receive glory and honor and power. For you created all things, and they exist because you created what you pleased."   —Revelation 19:9-11

Now that's what I call worship! When we worship God, we need to follow the examples of those who are in His presence—to worship Him continuously, enthusiastically, and in humility.

The natural response of every angel, demon, Satan, the heavenly host as well as all mankind (eventually) is to fall down in humility before the God of all creation. When Abraham saw God in Genesis 17, he fell on his face before Him. When Ezekiel witnessed God's glory, he fell on his face before Him. When Job realized it was God speaking to him from the mighty whirlwind, he said, "I abhor myself" (Job 42:6). When Daniel captured a glimpse of His glory, he passed out in fear. When the disciples heard God's voice on the

Mount of Olives in Matthew 17, they fell on their faces before Him.

Humility is the one characteristic that's drawn out of man when he appears before God. One day you'll know exactly what all these men felt. That's why the Bible says, "One day every knee shall bow and every tongue shall confess Jesus is Lord to the glory of the Father."

4. They are obeying His commands explicitly.

Praise the LORD, you his angels, you mighty ones who do his bidding, who obey his word. Praise the LORD, all his heavenly host, you his servants who do his will.

—Psalm 103:20

Jesus prayed a prayer in Matthew 6 that many people pray all over the earth. In that prayer, many people never realize a hidden truth. That truth is that everything done in heaven is according to the perfect will of God. Listen to what Jesus prayed and see if you haven't prayed this prayer as well and experienced the truth I've shared:

Our Father in heaven, hallowed be Your name. Your kingdom come. Your will be done on earth as it is in heaven. Give us this day our daily bread. And forgive us our debts, as we forgive our debtors. And do not lead us into temptation. But deliver us from the evil one. For Yours is the kingdom and the power and the glory forever. Amen.

—Matthew 6:9-13

In heaven, the angels and the heavenly host follow God's command explicitly!

What Are Angels Doing Here on Earth?

Angels are part of the "heavenly host" mentioned in the Bible. While the cherubim, the seraphim, and the four living beings were created to worship and serve God continuously before His throne in heaven, the angels have a separate mission. While angels are often seen in Scripture worshipping God before His throne, their mission goes beyond that, transcending the reaches of heaven with the purpose of assisting God in His work on earth. It's not because God needs their help. It's simply because God chooses to use them. God doesn't need the angels any more than He needs us. However, out of His love and divine plan, He chooses to use us to do His work on earth. He chooses to use the angels in the same way.

1. They are protecting us.

> For he will order his angels to protect you
> wherever you go.   —Psalm 91:11

God sent his angel to protect Daniel from hungry lions in the lion's den:

> My God sent his angel to shut the lions'
> mouths so that they would not hurt me, for I
> have been found innocent in his sight.
> —Daniel 6:22

God sent an angel to set Peter free from the bondage of a prison cell:

Suddenly, there was a bright light in the cell, and an angel of the Lord stood before Peter. The angel struck him on the side to awaken him and said, "Quick! Get up!" And the chains fell off his wrists. Then the angel told him, "Get dressed and put on your sandals." And he did. "Now put on your coat and follow me," the angel ordered. So Peter left the cell, following the angel. But all the time he thought it was a vision. He didn't realize it was actually happening. They passed the first and second guard posts and came to the iron gate leading to the city, and this opened for them all by itself. So they passed through and started walking down the street, and then the angel suddenly left him.

— Acts 12:7-10

2. They are guiding us.

The evangelist Philip was given directions by an angel:

As for Philip, an angel of the Lord said to him, "Go south down the desert road that runs from Jerusalem to Gaza." — Acts 8:26

3. They are influencing us.

Please remember there are two kinds of angels. First, there are the good angels who serve God. These are the angels we've been reviewing in this book so far. Secondly, there are bad angels. These angels followed Satan in his rebellion against God and now serve him in an effort to separate people from God.

Satan is still under God's ultimate authority as seen in Job 1, but he also realizes he's doomed to eternal destruction. That's why he's aligned his forces to take as many people with him as possible. Satan knows man is the apple of God's eye. He knows God loves us and desires the best for us. But because of his wickedness and pride, he continues to rebel against God. In that initiative, he's doing all he can to divert our attention from God. If he's doing that to you, ask for God's help today! God will deliver you from his attacks on your life, your marriage, your children, and your job.

Satan is not a god. He is a fallen, defeated being God created. He's headed for the Lake of Fire. His mission is to take you with him.

4. They are influencing world leaders.

Satan will also use national and world leaders to keep the truth of the gospel from ever getting to the people they rule. He will use these leaders like pawns on a chessboard to destroy as many people as possible. Look at what John wrote in Revelation 16:

> And I saw three evil spirits that looked like frogs leap from the mouths of the dragon, the beast and the false prophet. They are demonic spirits who work miracles and go out to all the rulers of the world to gather them for battle against the Lord on that great judgment day of God the Almighty.
> —Revelation 16:13-14

Keep in mind, this is *not* a battle between God and Satan. That battle was won by God some two thousand years ago when Jesus died and rose again from the grave, proving He is who He said He was. Satan knows he's defeated and doomed. He also knows he has a very short time (Revelation 12:12) to do his work. Because time is short, he has stepped up his efforts in an all-out battle to destroy marriages, destroy pastors and religious leaders, ruin world leaders with corruption and greed, and create depression, worry, anxiety, and stress in as many lives as he can. He is bent on a mission to turn people's trust away from God. To initiate his schemes, he will target world leaders.

> And the demonic spirits gathered all the rulers and their armies to a place with the Hebrew name Armageddon.
> —Revelation 16:16

The Bible reveals to us the reality of what's going on behind the scenes with many world leaders. In Daniel 10, we read the following again:

> Then he said, "Don't be afraid, Daniel. Since the first day you began to pray for understanding and to humble yourself before your God, your request has been heard in heaven. I have come in answer to your prayer. But for twenty-one days the spirit prince of the kingdom of Persia blocked my way. Then Michael, one of the archangels, came to help me, and I left him there with the spirit prince of the kingdom of Persia." —Daniel 10:12-13

It's important to note the angel was held captive—not by a human prince of Persia, but by Satan himself or a high-ranking demon who had authority to rule over the Persian kingdom. What this tells us is exactly what the apostle Paul said in Ephesians 6:12:

> For we are not fighting against flesh-and-blood enemies, but against evil rulers and authorities of the unseen world, against mighty powers in this dark world, and against evil spirits in the heavenly places.

While all these evil forces are actively working, please remember God's angels are actively working too! Rest assured, they are battling them and protecting nations and world rulers as well.

Notice how Michael, God's archangel, is the prince of Israel.

> Meanwhile, I will tell you what is written in the Book of Truth. No one helps me against these spirit princes except Michael, your spirit prince.   —Daniel 10:21

There are spirit princes over every kingdom in the world. I wonder what spirit prince is over America, over Britain, over Russia, over Australia . . . ? It makes you wonder, doesn't it?

5. They are influencing the natural elements of this world.

Revelation shows us some of the things angels have power to control, especially in the last days before the second coming of Christ.

For instance, they can hold back the winds of the earth.

Several types of winds blow around the earth: the prevailing winds, the easterly trade winds, the westerly trade winds, and the polar easterlies. These winds blow in specific directions, controlled by either high and low pressure systems or the earth's movements. To think God will one day ask His angels to hold back the wind movement on earth is an incredible thing indeed.

> Then I saw four angels standing at the four corners of the earth, holding back the four winds so they did not blow on the earth or the sea, or even on any tree.
>
> — Revelation 7:1

They can cause worldwide plagues.

> Then I heard a mighty voice from the Temple say to the seven angels, "Go your ways and pour out on the earth the seven bowls containing God's wrath." So the first angel left the Temple and poured out his bowl on the earth, and horrible, malignant sores broke out on everyone who had the mark of the beast and who worshiped his statue. Then the second angel poured out his bowl on the sea, and it became like the blood of a

corpse. And everything in the sea died. Then the third angel poured out his bowl on the rivers and springs, and they became blood. Then the fourth angel poured out his bowl on the sun, causing it to scorch everyone with its fire. Then the fifth angel poured out his bowl on the throne of the beast, and his kingdom was plunged into darkness. Then the sixth angel poured out his bowl on the great Euphrates River, and it dried up so that the kings from the east could march their armies toward the west without hindrance. Then the seventh angel poured out his bowl into the air. And a mighty shout came from the throne in the Temple, saying, "It is finished!" Then the thunder crashed and rolled, and lightning flashed. And a great earthquake struck—the worst since people were placed on the earth.

—Revelation 16:2-18

6. They are standing amazed at God's love for us.

In Ephesians 3 we read that one of the many purposes of God's interaction with us is to show His angels His love, mercy, forgiveness, grace, and wisdom.

God's purpose in all this was to use the church to display his wisdom in its rich variety to all the unseen rulers and authorities in the heavenly places.

—Ephesians 3:10

Peter, one of Jesus's disciples, even commented on how the angels are amazed at the "good news" of salvation through faith in Jesus Christ. You see, they stand in the holy presence of God and have witnessed His great judgment upon Satan and one-third of the angels who rebelled. They've witnessed God's hatred for sin. Now, when they look upon us in view of our sinful ways and see how disrespectful we are toward God, they are amazed that God doesn't wipe us off the map. Peter added how angels eagerly watch the manifold grace, mercy, and forgiveness of God at work in the lives of sinful men. They are "wowed" by God's love for man and His willingness to give us second chances, third chances, and so on.

And now this Good News has been announced to you by those who preached in the power of the Holy Spirit sent from heaven. It is all so wonderful that even the angels are eagerly watching these things happen. —1 Peter 1:12

7. They are transporting people to heaven and hell.

In Luke 16, Jesus tells a remarkable story of two men—one rich, the other a beggar. When they both died, the beggar was "carried by the angels" into a place called "Abraham's bosom." It was a temporary holding place for those who lived righteously before the Lord. When Jesus died on the cross and conquered death, hell, sin, and the grave, He took them from Abraham's bosom and into the very presence of almighty God—heaven!

So it was that the beggar died, and was carried by the angels to Abraham's bosom.

—Luke 16:22

Jesus also tells us in the Gospel of Matthew that the wicked will be carried by the angels as well; however, it will be to hell.

represent evil doctrines and those who spread them

Therefore as the tares are gathered and burned in the fire, so it will be at the end of this age. The Son of Man will send out His angels, and they will gather out of His kingdom all things that offend, and those who practice lawlessness, and will cast them into the furnace of fire. There will be wailing and gnashing of teeth. —Matthew 13:40-42

So our Lord tells us directly that angels are involved in the transport of our spirits into either heaven or hell.

What about Guardian Angels?

Every biblical scholar agrees that one of the duties of angels is to protect us. But what remains widely debated over thousands of years is the question, "Do each of us have a specific angel or angels assigned to protect us?" Many theologians have discussed this concept, but the question remains, "What does the Bible say?"

Before we explore what the Bible actually says on this topic, let's first look at *how* this concept arose to such prominence.

Let me offer a note of importance here. My intention is to seek truth. That compels me to look beyond church doctrine and old teachings to see what the Bible itself has to say about this issue.

Since angels do provide protection as ordered by God, maybe the rest of what I'm about to write isn't really that important. However, some of you reading this chapter may want to understand *why* the concept is prevalent and *what* the truth actually is.

Again, please note my intention is NOT to slander any religion or group of people as we dissect this issue. I have dear friends among all the groups I discuss below, and I respect them sincerely. For me, however, answering this question (because it is a prevalent thought among so many people) becomes more of a matter of seeking truth. We have to understand why this subject has become a major teaching in these religious circles and what the Bible actually says.

The question is not, "Do angels guard and protect us?" That answer is a resounding "Yes!"

The real question is, "Are specific angels assigned to us to protect us?"

Here's how *guardian angel* teaching has developed over the years:

Among Catholics:

The concept of each person having a guardian angel can be tracked down through antiquity. Even pagans such as Menander, Plutarch, and Plotinus held this view.

However, it first became a popular idea among early Christian historians such as Saint Jerome, a fourth-century Catholic priest who said, "The concept of guardian angels is in the 'mind of the

Church.'" He added, ". . . how great the dignity of the soul since each one has from his birth an angel commissioned to guard it."

Later, a prominent Catholic leader, Honorius of Autun, said every soul was assigned a guardian angel the moment it was put into a body. Later, Thomas Aquinas, another prominent Catholic leader, agreed with Honorius and believed it was the lowest order of angels who served as guardians. His view became very popular among Christians. Eventually, in the fifteenth century, the Feast of the Guardian Angels was added to the official calendar of Catholic holidays.

Eventually this concept became part of the Catechism of the Catholic Church (1992 AD) No. 336: From infancy to death, human life is surrounded by their watchful care and intercession. "Beside each believer stands an angel as protector and shepherd leading him to life."

Even as late as 2014, Pope Francis told those who gathered for the Feast of the Guardian Angels during the Morning Meditation in the chapel of Santa Marta that he had the feeling "I should do this, [or] this is not right, be careful." This, he said, "is the voice of our guardian angel . . ."

Pope Francis went on to say, "According to Church tradition we all have an angel with us, who guards us. . ." The pope instructed, "Do not rebel; follow his advice!" He urged that this "doctrine on the angels" not be considered "a little imaginative." It is rather one of "truth." It is "what Jesus, what God said, 'I send an angel before you, to guard you, to accompany you on the way so you will not make a mistake.'"

Disturbingly, however, Pope Francis made several statements that don't reflect the teachings of the Bible. At the conclusion of the Feast of the Guardian Angels, he urged his audience to ask a series of questions to help each person examine his or her own conscience: "How is my relationship with my guardian angel? Do I listen to him? Do I bid him good day in the morning? Do I tell him: 'guard me while I sleep?' Do I speak with him? Do I ask his advice? Is he beside me?. . .Each one of us can do so in order to evaluate the relationship with this angel that the Lord has sent to guard me and to accompany me on the path, and who always beholds the face of the Father who is in heaven."

Again, my intent is *not* to slander Pope Francis or the Catholic Church or its leadership in any way. My concern is this: What does the Bible really say about guardian angels? That should be your concern as well.

So what *does* the Bible say?

Before we get there, let's look at what Jewish theology teaches on this subject.

Among Jews:

In Rabbinic literature, the rabbis expressed the notion that there are indeed guardian angels appointed by Adonai to watch over people.

As one rabbi put it, "Our sages tell us that each mitzvah we do creates an angel that serves as a shield and protection for us. After our passing, these angels testify on our behalf before the Heavenly Courts. So in that sense, we create our own guardian angels."

Among Protestants:

Over the centuries, many Protestants have been divided in their thoughts regarding this subject. While all Catholics, Jews, and Protestant Christians believe in the protection of angels, many Protestant believers question what the Bible truly says about specific guardian angels assigned to each of us.

As you compare the claims of Scripture with the claims of early Christians, one thing is certain. God's Word is much less emphatic and dogmatic about the existence of specific guardian angels assigned to us. While it's easy to form a belief in guardian angels from the writings of men and church doctrine, it's much more difficult to form this belief from the writings of God.

Three passages that have provoked this concept:

There are really only three biblical passages that allude to the concept of guardian angels. Let's take a close look to help us reach the right conclusion on this widely debated topic.

1. In the first passage, King David offers the following:

> For he will order his angels to protect you wherever you go. They will hold you up with their hands so you won't even hurt your foot on a stone. You will trample upon lions and cobras; you will crush fierce lions and serpents under your feet! The LORD says, "I will rescue those who love me. I will protect those who trust in my name."
> — Psalm 91:11-13

It's important to read this passage carefully in context. First, it says God will "order his angels to protect you wherever you go." So it's obvious that one role of angels (though not every angel) is to protect us. However, this verse does not mention the role of a "guardian angel" for each of us individually. Yet many theologians have used this passage to mean exactly that.

2. In the second passage, Matthew — one of the twelve disciples — records Jesus as saying:

> Take heed that ye despise not one of these little ones; for I say unto you, that in heaven their angels do always behold the face of my Father which is in heaven. — Matthew 18:10

From this one passage, most people conclude we have a guardian angel. Those who hold this view point to the statement where Jesus says "their angels." This one verse has led to practically all church doctrines regarding guardian angels. I can easily see how this conclusion can be drawn. In fact, I've often used this verse to prove it. However, this is *not* what Jesus is saying.

A careful study of this chapter begins with Jesus sitting a child on His lap as He speaks to a crowd. If you take this verse literally, then Jesus informs us that guardian angels are only with children. However, that's not the case either.

We must take a broader look at the scriptures about angels. That's how you form a correct doctrinal position. When you take one scripture and form a belief system around it out of context, you can be led down a wrong path. Cultists are known for this type of practice.

129

When we do take a broader look at the entire Bible, we see an undeniable fact: We are surrounded by the presence of angels. Angels are everywhere. To use this single verse to prove how this young child has guardian angels assigned to him isn't the most accurate exegesis of this verse.

Is it possible there are specific angels assigned to us? Yes! But here's what Jesus is simply stating: This child (as well as every believer) has angels who stand in the presence of God. God sees what goes on around us. If the angels wanted to, they could easily deliver a message about us directly to the throne of God the Father.

In effect, Jesus is warning His listeners that angels are all around believers, beholding us, observing us, and if need be they can take their observations straight to the throne room of the Almighty.

While holy angels cannot and will not do anything without a command sent from God the Father, they can bring observations to Him!

3. The third passage is found in the book of Acts chapter 12. On this particular occasion, one of Jesus's disciples, Peter, was arrested and thrown in jail for proclaiming his belief in Jesus as the long-awaited Jewish Messiah.

While locked securely within the confines of that prison cell, God sent an angel to rescue him. As the angel led Peter out of the prison and through the gates of the city, Peter made his way to the house of Mary, the mother of John Mark. As he knocked on the door repeatedly, a young girl named Rhoda came to answer. After hearing Peter's cry for help, she excitedly ran back into a room full of guests and said, "Peter is at the door!" She was so excited she literally forgot to open the door to let Peter in!

The guests, however, knew the serious situation Peter was in. They knew he was securely locked up in jail and doubted he was at the door of their own house. The probability of that was zero. By this time, they assumed he had died.

It was their response to Rhoda that's led many people since then to believe we have at least one guardian angel. Here's what these Jewish guests said:

> "You're out of your mind," they told her. When she kept insisting that it was so, they said, "It must be his angel."   — Acts 12:15

When you read this passage, you can easily conclude how these Jews believed it was Peter's guardian angel. They used the Greek word *angelos*, meaning "angel." But before you draw a definitive conclusion about this passage teaching us about guardian angels, please keep in mind two very important things.

First, the *only* Scripture the Jewish people had at that time was the Septuagint—the Old Testament. The New Testament hadn't been written yet. The only place in the Old Testament where you could potentially conclude the possibility of each person having a guardian angel is Psalm 91:11-13, the passage we discussed above. However, this passage does not specifically teach us to draw that definitive conclusion.

Secondly, despite the fact the Old Testament never specifically teaches that we each have a guardian angel, it was a longstanding traditional doctrine of Judaism. Every Jew has a guardian angel—that's what they taught. In fact, Judaism teaches that each Jew has at least two guardian angels assigned to them. Keep in mind, though, that no scripture in the entire Bible actually teaches this.

But if my deductive reasoning skills are in error (along with other theologians who agree) and we do have guardian angels assigned to us, then I say, "Praise the Lord!"

If you've had an experience with God's angels protecting you, guiding you, or helping you in any way, I'd love to hear about it. Visit my book's website at **www.AngelsUTM.com** and tell us your story! It could be an encouragement and a blessing to so many people.

Chapter 7

Other Spiritual Beings You Should Know About

As you stroll through the Bible, you'll notice mention of several types of spiritual beings. Angels just happen to be one of them. While most people believe in the existence of angels, many aren't aware of the other spiritual beings God has created.

Some of these beings may seem strange, but they're an important part of God's plan and overall design. Since the Bible gives us more information about the angels than any other heavenly being, we have spent more time on them. But it's significant that God took the time to reveal through His Word other important beings He wants us to know about.

When the Bible speaks of the "heavenly host," I believe it's referring to more than just angels. Angels are obviously a part of the heavenly host, but most people look at the heavenly host as being only angels. Not so!

Praise him, all his angels; praise him, all his
heavenly host.   —Psalm 148:2

Suddenly a great company of the heavenly
host appeared with the angel, praising God.
                                     —Luke 2:13

God's heavenly host includes angels, but He
has created other spiritual beings as well. They
serve a different purpose than that of angels. While
angels primarily serve as "servants," "ministering
spirits," and "messengers" to believers, the other
spiritual beings don't have a mission involving
believers. Their mission is confined to the throne of
God in heaven.

Let's begin with those beings for now.

Those who serve before God's throne.

The human mind simply cannot conceive of
the glory of God on His throne and the incredible
opportunity these spiritual beings have! In fact,
Moses asked God one day if he could get a glimpse
of Him in all His glory. This is what God told
Moses, which would be true for you and me today:

Moses responded, "Then show me your
glorious presence." The LORD replied, "I will
make all my goodness pass before you, and
I will call out my name, Yahweh, before you.
For I will show mercy to anyone I choose,
and I will show compassion to anyone I
choose. But you may not look directly at my
face, for no one may see me and live."
                                     —Exodus 33:18-20

Imagine that! No man can see God's face and live.

God's glory is so great and His holiness so pure, no man could ever stand before Him and survive. Our sinful nature prohibits that. Great men of the Bible have captured glimpses of His nearly indescribable glory. Look what happened:

- When Moses saw a glimpse of His glory, he fell on his knees and buried his face in the dirt, terrified of what he saw.
- Isaiah cried out, "Woe is me! For I am unclean!"
- Ezekiel passed out.
- Daniel said, "My strength left me."
- John said, "I fell at His feet as a dead man."

The natural response of every man in the Bible was to immediately fall down in fear and reverence as they witnessed God's amazing glory. That's why the Bible prophesies of a future day when "every knee shall bow and every tongue confess that Jesus is Lord, to the glory of the Father."

God promises there's going to be a day in the future when all men—everyone who has ever lived—will stand before Him and give an accounting for their lives. He also promises that regardless of who they are, whatever their status in life was, it doesn't matter. Every person will fall before His holy and powerful presence and confess that Jesus is the mighty Son of God. All of this is for one purpose: to give glory to Him. God has tried throughout the ages to get man's attention. On that day, He will get it.

Now let's take a closer look at those whose mission is to stay before the throne of God at all times.

When you read the Bible chronologically beginning with the book of Genesis, the very first spiritual beings you see that God created are the cherubim, whose name means "to guard."

1. The cherubim.

The cherubim are mentioned several times throughout the Old Testament and once in the New Testament. The first time is Genesis 3. When Adam and Eve sinned by eating from the forbidden tree (the tree of knowledge of good and evil), God banished them from the Garden of Eden and stationed powerful cherubim to guard against them ever coming back.

> After sending them out, the LORD God stationed mighty cherubim to the east of the Garden of Eden. And he placed a flaming sword that flashed back and forth to guard the way to the tree of life.   —Genesis 3:4

The next time we see the word *cherubim* in the Bible is the book of Exodus, where God commands Moses to build a tabernacle along with some furniture to go into it. Each piece of furniture had a powerful symbolic meaning. One of those pieces of furniture was the Ark of the Covenant. You probably remember hearing about it in the famous movie *Raiders of the Lost Ark*.

The Ark of the Covenant was approximately 45 inches long, 27 inches wide, and 27 inches high. It contained a lid that was called the Mercy Seat or place of atonement. In type, it represents the throne of God.

The entire ark was covered with gold. Atop the lid were formed two cherubim, each facing each other with their wings spread out and their wing tips touching each other, with the cherubim looking down upon the Mercy Seat. The Mercy Seat is where God would speak to Moses during those days in the desert.

In heaven, the cherubim surround the throne of God where God sits right above them. In Isaiah 37:16, King Hezekiah prays, addressing God as "enthroned above the cherubim."

So what do cherubim look like?

From Ezekiel chapter 1, we see Ezekiel trying to describe these very unusual-looking creatures. First, there are four of them in number, and they have the appearance of a man. Secondly, they have four wings. However, when looking into their faces, Ezekiel notices something strikingly unique. Each being has four faces: the face of a man, a lion, an ox, and an eagle. Thirdly, Ezekiel describes them as having straight legs with feet much like the hoof of a calf. When they moved, they did so in a straightforward direction. They only moved as the Spirit led them. Fourthly, fire moved back and forth among the cherubim.

Take a look at these verses in Ezekiel:

. . . and in the fire was what looked like four living creatures. In appearance their form was human, but each of them had four faces

and four wings. Their legs were straight; their feet were like those of a calf and gleamed like burnished bronze. Under their wings on their four sides they had human hands. All four of them had faces and wings, and the wings of one touched the wings of another. Each one went straight ahead; they did not turn as they moved. Their faces looked like this: Each of the four had the face of a human being, and on the right side each had the face of a lion, and on the left the face of an ox; each also had the face of an eagle. Such were their faces. They each had two wings spreading out upward, each wing touching that of the creature on either side; and each had two other wings covering its body. Each one went straight ahead. Wherever the spirit would go, they would go, without turning as they went. The appearance of the living creatures was like burning coals of fire or like torches. Fire moved back and forth among the creatures; it was bright, and lightning flashed out of it. The creatures sped back and forth like flashes of lightning.
—Ezekiel 1:5-14

A few chapters later in Ezekiel 10, we find these living creatures are actually called "cherubim." Later, in Ezekiel 28, we find more specific information about these majestic beings. However, if you're not an astute Bible student, you would probably miss the point of this chapter.

In Ezekiel 28, God is giving a prophecy to Ezekiel about the king of Tyre. What's important to keep in mind in this chapter is this: The first ten verses are directed at the human side of the king of Tyre. It refers to the actual man who ran the country of Tyre. But in verses 11-19, God provides an additional prophecy that takes a different direction. It is solely directed to the evil spirit behind the actions, thoughts, and heart of the king of Tyre. That evil spirit is Satan.

If you're not careful, you'll miss this critically important difference. Keep in mind that the Bible teaches us in Ephesians 6: "For our struggle is not against flesh and blood, but against the rulers, against the authorities, against the powers of this dark world and against the spiritual forces of evil in the heavenly realms."

If you'll keep that in mind, it's not difficult to see the transition here. Now God is addressing Satan, who was one of the cherubim before he was kicked out of heaven.

How do we know God is addressing Satan? Simple! We know the actual human form of the king of Tyre was never in the Garden of Eden as mentioned in verse 13, but Satan was. We know he was never ordained and anointed as "the mighty angelic guardian," but Satan was. We also know the human form of the king of Tyre never "walked among the stones of fire" which are in heaven, but Satan did. Plus, numerous other passages of the Bible show how Satan and his demonic forces are actively working to control the leaders of nations all around the world.

From the passage in Ezekiel 28:11-19, we therefore learn some very interesting and alarming things. God reminded Satan of his former glory and the sin that drove him from "the mount of God" and from God's glorious presence.

Perhaps most importantly, we learn from this passage that Satan was once a part of the cherubim. How beautiful he was created to be! In fact, God reminds him of his former glory:

> You were the model of perfection, full of wisdom and exquisite in beauty. You were in Eden, the garden of God. Your clothing was adorned with every precious stone: red carnelian, pale-green peridot, white moonstone blue-green beryl, onyx, green jasper, blue lapis lazuli, turquoise, and emerald all beautifully crafted for you and set in the finest gold. They were given to you on the day you were created. I ordained and anointed you as the mighty angelic guardian. You had access to the holy mountain of God and walked among the stones of fire. You were blameless in all you did from the day you were created until the day evil was found in you. Your rich commerce led you to violence, and you sinned. So I banished you in disgrace from the mountain of God. I expelled you, O mighty guardian, from your place among the stones of fire. Your heart was filled with pride because of all your beauty. Your wisdom was corrupted by your love of splendor. So I threw you to the ground and exposed you to the curious gaze of kings. You defiled your sanctuaries with your many sins and your dishonest trade. So I brought fire out from within you, and it consumed you. I reduced you to ashes on the ground in the sight of all who were watching. All who knew you are appalled at

your fate. You have come to a terrible end, and you will exist no more.

—Ezekiel 28:11-19

We can conclude from these verses that the cherubim have the following characteristics:

- They are a "model of perfection."
- They are "full of wisdom and exquisite in beauty."
- They are "adorned with every precious stone...beautifully crafted..."
- They were given this beauty "on the day you were created."
- They were ordained and anointed "as the mighty angelic guardian."
- They had "access to the holy mountain of God."

In addition to this description God gives in Ezekiel 28, the prophet describes them even further in the first chapter of the book that bears his name. Ezekiel speaks of them initially as "the four living creatures." Later, in chapter 10, he refers to them as cherubim. Here's a little bit of what he adds to their looks, characteristics, and purpose found in Ezekiel 1:5-13:

- They are "four" in number.
- They have "four wings."
- The have "four faces."
- Each pair of wings is "stretched out to touch the wings of the living beings on either side of it."
- The other pair of wings "covered its body."

- Under each wing are "human hands."
- Their legs "are straight" and their feet are like the hoof "of a calf."
- Each has the face of a man, a lion, an ox, and an eagle.
- They give off a radiance that appears as "brilliant torches."
- "Lightning seemed to flash back and forth among them."
- They "darted to and fro like flashes of lightning."
- Ezekiel also records them as having "wheels" that "sparkled as if made of beryl" with a frightening appearance whereas the rims were "covered with eyes all around" with a "second wheel turning crosswise within it."
- When they flew, Ezekiel records the powerful sound of the wings as being "like the voice of the Almighty or like the shouting of a mighty army."

As strange and incredible as this description might sound, these are the cherubim who stand before the very presence of God. Only God knows why He made them this way, yet the Bible teaches that they are absolutely awesome in beauty, radiance, and glory. I'm sure Ezekiel was fearful as he looked upon them, yet amazed at the wonder of their construction.

As far as angelic-like creatures go, the cherubim are one of the highest order in their duties before God. Their function is different from that of angels, yet they do all that God commands. They bask in His glory and give Him glory all day long. They are the throne-bearers of God. They give Him continual praise. And they follow each of His commands.

The next spiritual beings we read about that are continually in the presence of God are the seraphim.

2. The seraphim.

Unfortunately, the Bible mentions the seraphim only once, in Isaiah chapter 6. The word *seraph* means "burning one." They are quite different from the cherubim because they have six wings instead of four. Two wings are used to cover their face, two are used to cover their feet, and two are used to fly. While the cherubim do not use their wings to fly since they follow the Spirit within the wheels, the seraphim use wings for mobility. Their purpose is to fly above and around the throne of God shouting thunderous praise to Him. Isaiah records them as crying out to one another, "Holy, holy, holy is the Lord of Heaven's Armies! The whole earth is filled with his glory!" This is similar to the "Four Living Beings" mentioned in the book of Revelation, yet they are vastly different in design.

Isaiah was astounded by how loud and powerful their voices were. He said their voices shook the very "Temple of God to its foundations."

Seeing and experiencing all of this, Isaiah felt a great disparity between the indescribable holiness of God and his sinfulness as a man. Immediately upon experiencing the loud shouts of the seraphim and realizing he was in the midst of God's holy presence, he cries out, "I am doomed, for I am a sinful man. I have filthy lips, and I live among a people with filthy lips."

I have no doubt this is exactly what every single one of us will feel one day as we stand in the presence of the holy God! The Bible tells us in Romans 14:11-12, "For the Scriptures say, 'As surely as I live,' says the LORD, 'every knee will bend to me, and every tongue will declare allegiance to God. Yes, each of us will give a personal account to God.'"

Throughout the Scriptures, there are numerous occasions when men and women see an angel. As a result, their natural response is great fear. That's what happened to Mary and Joseph, the human parents of Jesus. But when godly men like Ezekiel (Ezekiel 1:28) and the apostle John (Revelation 1:17) were given the unique privilege of catching a glimpse of God's glory, their natural response was to fall forward in great fear and humility. In fact, John records that he fell at His feet "like a dead man."

On the occasion when Moses begged to see God in all His glory, in fact, God responded (in Exodus 33:20): "But you may not look directly at my face, for no one may see me and live."

God is so holy that no man in our current sinful state can see God and live. One day, everyone shall look upon Him and see Him in His glory. On that day, all men will know beyond any doubt the reality of His holiness, greatness, and the vast expanse of His infinite power! It will be the natural response of all of us to bow before Him. I hope you'll understand that now before it is too late!

I agree with one old preacher who used to say, "You may not want to bow your knee to Him now, but one day you will. And you'll do it willingly, naturally, without any hesitation, and you'll be so convinced of who He is that before it even crosses

your conscious mind, you will have confessed on
your own tongue your allegiance to Him as the one
true God. It will be the natural response of all men
who stand in His wonderful presence."

It's interesting to note that Isaiah, feeling the
conviction of his own sinfulness before a holy
God and unable to speak, was approached by one
of the seraphim with a burning coal from off the
altar (Isaiah 6:6). Once the live coal was pressed
to his lips to purify his lips, he could then speak
before God.

The purpose of the seraphim is to give glory
and praise to God continuously and to obey His
commands explicitly.

3. The four living beings.

The other spiritual beings we see in Scripture
who stay in the presence of God and offer Him
nonstop worship are the four living beings
mentioned in Revelation chapter 4:

> In front of the throne was a shiny sea of
> glass, sparkling like crystal. In the center
> and around the throne were four living
> beings, each covered with eyes, front and
> back. The first of these living beings was like
> a lion; the second was like an ox; the third
> had a human face; and the fourth was like
> an eagle in flight. Each of these living beings
> had six wings, and their wings were covered
> all over with eyes, inside and out. Day after
> day and night after night they keep on
> saying, "Holy, holy, holy is the Lord God, the

Almighty — the one who always was, who is,
and who is still to come." — Revelation 4:6-8

Some scholars suggest the four living beings
could be the same as the seraphim since they have
six wings and cry out the same praise before God.
Still others think they might be the cherubim found
in the book of Ezekiel since they're referred to as
"four living creatures." However, there is a notice-
able difference between the two.

There are several things to keep in mind that
prove their difference from the seraphim. They
are similar to seraphim in having six wings and
in crying out to God in the same manner, true. But
it's important to note that Isaiah saw them as being
"above" the throne of God. These four living beings
are in the "center and around" God's throne.

Regarding their difference from cherubim,
remember that cherubim are "below" the throne
and have only four wings, not six.

Another unique characteristic distinguishing
the four living beings from the cherubim is this:
The cherubim look like a human being but have
four faces (a man, a lion, an ox, and an eagle). In
Revelation, the four living beings are described as
four beings, not having four faces, but one being
looking like a man, one looking like a lion, one
looking like an ox, and the fourth looking like an
eagle. John, in Revelation, did not see these beings
as human with four faces, but rather as four distinct
beings looking like the four faces of the cherubim.

I know this might sound confusing, but after
digesting all the characteristics of these beings, it's
my conclusion that they are three distinct beings.

Someone might say, "Well, perhaps John didn't quite get it right. Or perhaps Ezekiel was wrong about the number of the wings."

I don't think so. God allowed them to write with clarity and to remember exactly what they saw. While man can make a mistake, God can't. He allowed these men to write down exactly what they saw. He has preserved His Word throughout the ages.

So let's see if we can correctly picture the spiritual beings before the throne of God.

As we look to the throne of God, we see the cherubim possessing indescribable beauty. They're seated at the foot of the throne providing God continuous worship with their perfect voices of praise. As our eyes adjust to the center of the throne, we see the four living beings who bear the resemblance of the cherubim with four faces, but also closely resemble the seraphim with six wings and their cries of glorious, thunderous praise over God's holiness. As we glance upward to the top of the throne near the face of God, we see the seraphim flying around the throne offering loud, thunderous praises to God. They use two wings to cover their faces, two wings to cover their feet, and two to fly as they bask in God's glory.

Wow, what a sight that must be!

The question people sometimes ask me is, "Randy, do you think there might be more spiritual beings than what the Bible teaches us?"

My answer to that is "Yes!"

Jesus made an interesting statement in John 3:12 to Nicodemus, one of the most prominent religious leaders of His time: "But if you don't believe me when I tell you about earthly things, how can you possibly believe if I tell you about heavenly things?"

It's as though Jesus were asking, "Hey, if you can't really trust Me about the simple things of earth, then how will you ever be able to comprehend heavenly things?" God only gives us what we need to know. There's only so much we can understand. Much of what I've shared in this book sounds so farfetched that many people just can't believe in cherubim, seraphim, or even a spiritual world at all. Our minds are limited in what we can trust and hold to be true. Our minds are conditioned by the restraints of a physical world.

Those who work on earth.

First, it's important to realize there are ranks of angels, not only among God's holy angels, but among demons as well. To understand this concept, you have to understand that God is a God of order and purpose. When God created the world, He did so with order and purpose. God is the top of that hierarchy. So it follows that there's a ranking system throughout the spiritual world similar to our military.

When God created the animals, He gave man dominion over them. When God created man, He gave man the responsibility to lead his wife and family. That's because God is a God of order and purpose.

When He created the spirit world, He created it with order and purpose. In fact, several verses in the Bible allude to the ranks of powers within the spiritual world:

> For through him God created everything in
> the heavenly realms and on earth. He made
> the things we can see and the things we can't
> see—such as thrones, kingdoms, rulers and
> authorities in the unseen world. Everything
> was created through Him and for Him.
> —Colossians 1:16

Notice what Paul says below:

> For we are not fighting against flesh-and-
> blood enemies, but against evil rulers and
> authorities of the unseen world, against
> mighty powers in this dark world, and
> against evil spirits in the heavenly places.
> —Ephesians 6:12

Paul provides us insight into the fact that evil
rulers and authorities are uniquely positioned
within the spiritual world. In that same verse,
he goes on to say that we fight against "mighty
powers" and "evil spirits" in the heavenly places.
Now look at what Peter said:

> Now Christ has gone to heaven. He is seated
> in the place of honor next to God, and all the
> angels and authorities and powers accept
> His authority.   —1 Peter 3:22

I find it interesting how Peter speaks of three
distinct ranks within the spiritual world. He first
mentions that "angels" accept the authority of
Jesus Christ. Then he cites how "authorities" accept
Jesus's supreme authority. Then he mentions that
"powers" do as well.

While God doesn't give us more information than that, we can certainly see that He has created everything with order and purpose and a definite ranking of power within the angelic realm.

The archangel of God.

In the ranking system God has instituted, there is one angel who provides oversight over other angels. This angel also provides oversight regarding the events that take place within a nation or some geographical territory on earth. This angel of great strength and authority is called an "archangel." The term or prefix *arch* is Greek for "ruling" or "chief."

Strangely enough, only one archangel is mentioned in the Bible. His name is Michael. The only angel in the entire Bible to whom the term archangel is applied is Michael.

> At that time Michael, the archangel who stands guard over your nation, will arise.
> —Daniel 12:1

However, the Jews and many others have considered Gabriel as one of the archangels as well. While Gabriel is never mentioned as an archangel in the Bible, the Jews assume he is because he announces that he stands in the very presence of God.

> Then the angel said, "I am Gabriel! I stand in the very presence of God. It was he who sent me to bring you this good news!"
> —Luke 1:19

In fact, a strong Jewish tradition claims there are seven archangels. According to Jewish tradition, the seven archangels are Michael, Gabriel, Raphael, Uriel, Raguel, Sarakiel, and Phanuel. However, you can't find anything in the Bible that teaches the existence of seven archangels or even their names.

Even though Michael is the only archangel specifically mentioned in the Bible, a verse in Daniel seems to imply there may be more than one. Look at Daniel 10:13:

> But for twenty-one days the spirit prince of the kingdom of Persia blocked my way. Then Michael, one of the archangels, came to help me.

Notice Michael is "one of the archangels." Or as other versions state, "one of the chief princes." And, in another passage, the Bible says the following:

> But even Michael, one of the mightiest of the angels, did not dare accuse the devil of blasphemy, but simply said, "The Lord rebuke you!"   —Jude 1:9

Since he is one of "the mightiest of the angels," the question becomes, "Who are the other mightiest of angels?" In fact, John records in Revelation seven angels who stood in the presence of God, just like Gabriel. Could this be where Judaism concludes the existence of seven archangels?

> I saw the seven angels who stand before God, and they were given seven trumpets.
>   —Revelation 8:2

For the Lord himself will come down from heaven with a commanding shout, with the voice of the archangel, and with the trumpet call of God. First, the believers who have died will rise from their graves. Then, together with them, we who are still alive and remain on the earth will be caught up in the clouds to meet the Lord in the air. Then we will be with the Lord forever.

—1 Thessalonians 4:15-17

1. Lucifer/Satan

Lucifer (or Satan) was originally one of the highest spiritual beings ever created. He was one of the cherubim. However, the beauty and power God gave him went to his head. Being lifted up in his own pride, Satan desired to be worshipped just like the God who created him.

When God saw that His heart was corrupted, He cast him out of heaven and sent him hurling to the earth (see Ezekiel 28:18; Matthew 25:41). In his power, Satan was able to convince about one-third of God's angels to follow in his rebellion (Revelation 12:4). These rebellious angels are called demons or evil spirits.

Since a lot more information will be given in another chapter about this fascinating but tragic spiritual being, let's just suffice it to say (for now) that Satan is another spiritual being you must be aware of and understand.

2. Demons

Demons were originally created as angels. They were created holy like God, and they originally worshipped God. However, these angels were corrupted under the powerful influence of Satan, formerly called Lucifer by God. Since God drove Satan and these angels out of heaven and away from His presence, they are often called "fallen angels." Other names ascribed to them are "evil spirits," "demons," and "powers of the air."

The next chapter will explain more about these beings—another species you need to know about.

3. The imprisoned angels

Demons aren't the only fallen angels. Imprisoned angels are probably the worst of the worst. They did something no other demon had ever done before. Their sin was so horrible in the sight of God that He banished them and imprisoned them in hell. They have been chained up since that day. They cannot escape. However, God will one day in the future release them for a short time to create havoc in the world just before the second coming of Jesus.

So what was their sin? Sexual immorality!

> Then the people began to multiply on the earth, and daughters were born to them. The sons of God saw the beautiful women and took any they wanted as their wives.
> —Genesis 6:1-2

Who were these sons of God? And why did their children from the daughters of men grow into a race of giants? The three primary views on the identity of the sons of God are:

- They were fallen angels.
- They were powerful human rulers.
- They were godly descendants of Seth inter-
marrying with wicked descendants of Cain.

The first theory is given weight in the Old
Testament by the phrase "sons of Gods" always
referring to angels (Job 1:6; 2:1; 38:7). The fact
that these angels mated with human females has
a strong contextual, grammatical, and historical
basis. Even the famous Jewish historian Flavius
Josephus agrees—along with Philo, Eusebius, and
many other famous writers, historians, and theologians of early biblical history.

Note what's written in the book of Jude:

> And I remind you of the angels who did not
> stay within the limits of authority God gave
> them but left the place where they belonged.
> God has kept them securely chained in
> prisons of darkness, waiting for the great
> day of judgment.   —Jude 1:6

These angels exceeded the boundaries of their
authority. They abandoned their heavenly bodies
and their spiritual state in the heavenlies. As
mentioned earlier, angels have the ability to go
from the spiritual realm into the physical realm
and can quickly materialize into human form.
These rebellious angels decided to leave their
heavenly bodies and become like men to have
sexual relations with women.

God was so angry at their sin that, unlike other
demons that now roam the earth, He imprisoned
them in hell.

For God did not spare even the angels who sinned. He threw them into hell, in gloomy pits of darkness, where they are being held until the day of judgment.   — 2 Peter 2:4

Chapter 8

The Secrets of Fallen Angels

Although most Americans believe in angels, many are skeptical about fallen angels or demons as they're often called in the Bible. Some people see these concepts as folklore. But look around — you'll see plenty of TV programs, movies, video games, and other forms of entertainment that feature demons, ghosts, zombies, vampires, and all things evil. They've become very popular these days, especially with our youth.

I remember when I was in fifth grade, some of the kids in our church decided it would be fun to do a séance. Imagine, church kids dabbling in the occult! We didn't know what we were doing. We were just having fun as kids. But even the things that appear to be fun can be very dangerous. They can open the door for the kind of spirit you don't want, nor the kind you're seeking.

Later as a high school student, my friends and I decided we would visit a few haunted houses during Halloween. It was the 1970s, and haunted houses were just starting to become popular, especially among those with a profit motive.

Professional costumes and state-of-the-art effects were starting to take hold. For a kid looking for an adrenaline high, a haunted house seemed like a good way to go.

After attending a couple of them one night, I started to feel uneasy. I didn't mind talking skeletons or monsters jumping out at me, but seeing people dressed up as demons or demon-possessed people left me wondering, "Is this really the right thing to do?"

We were headed to our final haunted house for the night, and I told my friends how I was feeling. I just didn't want to do it anymore. They shrugged off my comments and assured me we were just having fun. So I went ahead and attended the last haunted house on our list.

That one changed everything for me. It was very scary with all the regular stuff such as dead people, coffins, bloody hands, spider webs, and such. Initially it was like all the others—until we got to the second floor. We crammed into a room where a girl was lying on a bed. The next thing I saw was a guy with a Bible trying to exorcise a demon out of her. She spewed something out of her mouth, started to shake almost uncontrollably, and roared with a sound that made the hairs on the back of my neck rise.

Although the whole thing was an act meant to scare people, it looked and seemed very real. As the girl kicked and screamed, I could feel in my heart that this was no place for me. Strangely, out of the dozen people in that small room that night, the demon-possessed girl came toward me. Her makeup made her look contorted as though some demon had claimed her. She came up close to my face. Before I could flee the room she pointed her finger at me and said, "I want to possess you!" She said this several times. I was done!

Quickly, I headed down the hallway, down the stairs, and angrily stormed toward the back door. Just before I left the house, a guy in a gorilla suit jumped out at me. I was so mad I instinctively punched him in the nose. He wasn't a gorilla any longer. He was just a teenage guy under a gorilla suit saying, "Hey, man, it's a joke!"

Right then and there, I was finished with haunted houses.

I told my dad what had happened and he agreed with me. I'll never forget what he said to me: "Son, you don't need to go looking for the devil, he knows where you live. And if you play in his backyard, you might get burned."

He was right. I was allowing all these things — haunted houses, scary movies, and demonic-styled games — to provide cheap thrills for me. I used to like the feeling of fear. All adrenaline junkies do to some degree. But then I remembered the following verse in the Bible:

For God has not given us a spirit of fear, but of power and of love and of a sound mind.
—2 Timothy 1:7

Fear doesn't come from God. It comes from Satan. The spirit of fear is a demonic spirit. When it overtakes you, it can paralyze you, throw you into depression, kill your confidence, and ultimately ruin your life. Fear comes from a lack of faith in God.

Notice the spirit God gives in that verse. It's one of power, love, and a sound mind. If there's anything we're all looking for, it's those three things. We're all looking for strength as we face the challenges of life. We're all looking for love and the feeling of being sincerely desired and appreciated. We're also all looking for a mind at peace, both with God and with man.

After all, which would you rather have?

I don't want to spend a lot of time talking about demons. I just want you to know enough to understand how they can influence your life in ways you're not thinking of—and how you can defeat them.

What the Bible tells us about demons.

First, demons are angels. Actually, they are the former angels of God. They're often called "the fallen angels." In other words, they were kicked out of heaven when they joined Satan's rebellion against God. Revelation tells us about one-third of the angels followed Satan and fell from the presence of God down to earth.

In the Bible, demons are also called "evil spirits," "unclean spirits," a "devil," a "lying spirit," and a "familiar spirit."

Under the command of Satan, demons know their end is eternal damnation in the Lake of Fire. As we approach the season of what many Bible scholars refer to as "the last days," these demons will become more active, knowing they have a short time. In fact, John records the words of an angel crying out in the book of Revelation:

> Woe to the inhabitants of the earth and the
> sea! For the devil has come down to you,
> having great wrath, because he knows that
> he has a short time.   —Revelation 12:12

I believe what we see in Jesus's day in terms
of demon possession is very typical of our day—
maybe even worse. We just don't realize it, nor are
we looking for it. We can't see beyond the surface
of the physical plane and witness all the dark forces
at work. But we can see their influence in this world
as we move the needle of morality farther away
from the holy desires of God. Each day we wake up
to the reality of evil all around us. When I speak of
evil, I'm not just talking about ISIS and the behead-
ings in the Middle East, or even what Hamas is
doing to Israel. We see the thumbprint of evil in the
little things all around us.

Demons and their strategies.

Demons have many strategies they use to their
advantage to ultimately draw your attention away
from God. They've had thousands of years to
perfect their craft. Look what Paul says about their
strategy in using a lack of forgiveness:

> I have forgiven that one for your sakes in the
> presence of Christ, lest Satan should take
> advantage of us; for we are not ignorant of
> his devices.   —2 Corinthians 2:10

Is there anyone you need to forgive? If so, don't
let the demons have victory in staging a hardened

heart toward someone. The way of God is always being willing to forgive.

> Make allowance for each other's faults, and forgive anyone who offends you. Remember, the Lord forgave you, so you must forgive others. —Colossians 3:13

The Bible tells us there are many other strategies demons use, and they usually begin with mind games. Instead of telling you how God sees you (which is the most important thing), they'll work hard to create a perception that makes you feel like you don't measure up to others. They'll tell you you're fat, ugly, skinny, nerdy, stupid, or unlovable. They want you to dwell on all the negative features the world can conceive so that you can blame God for how He made you. They may even do the opposite and tell you you're awesome, smart, talented, and beautiful—anything to make you feel self-sufficient so you don't need God.

Demons are con artists and liars. They will do everything they can to convince you there's nothing wrong with cheating, lying, adultery, fornication, stealing, murder, depression, oppression, hatred, and many other unlawful or sinful actions.

Demons love to infect the mind. It's their primary target. They will put things in your mind that have the potential to destroy your marriage—even the stupidest things. They encourage disobedience in young people. They love the drug and alcohol culture. They will use anything and do anything to bring harm to you personally, rob you of joy, fill you with anger, bring on jealousies, encourage mental deceptions that bring about depression, and cause conflict in your relationships. They want you to experience the worst of what life is all about. They work in every way that's contrary to God. They want to rob you of all that God desires to give you. And they work overtime to do it!

Demons will allow you to have fun but will rob you of inner joy and peace. They will allow you to enjoy the pleasures of life but will leave you with a great sense of emptiness. They'll offer you money, a great job, and anything else that could potentially interfere with your seeing your need for God. Keeping you from having a relationship with God is their ultimate drive and mission.

Someone once said, "An idle mind is the devil's workshop." So is a hectic schedule. I know too many well-meaning Christians who are so heavily involved in going to ballgames, soccer games, etc., they simply don't have time to enjoy God's Word, be faithful to church, or even pray. Slowly, their faith erodes. When they look back, they wonder, "What happened?"

Since we have a sinful nature that works against us as well, letting down your guard just a little can create an opportunity for demons to plant a seed in your mind that may eventually turn anger into hatred, concern into worry, frustration into depression, and marital discord into divorce.

Never let this happen to you!

The reality of demon possession.

When you read about the life of Jesus in the first four books of the New Testament (the Gospels), it's startling how often Jesus and His disciples were called to cast out demons. They encountered demon activity in both the young and old everywhere they traveled. Read the verses below and see just how often Jesus confronted this issue:

> That evening many demon-possessed people were brought to Jesus. He cast out the evil spirits with a simple command, and he healed all the sick. —Matthew 8:16

> When Jesus arrived on the other side of the lake, in the region of the Gadarenes, two men who were possessed by demons met him. They lived in a cemetery and were so violent that no one could go through that area.
> —Matthew 8:28

> Then a demon-possessed man, who was blind and couldn't speak, was brought to Jesus. He healed the man so that he could both speak and see. —Matthew 12:22

> A Gentile woman who lived there came to him, pleading, "Have mercy on me, O Lord, Son of David! For my daughter is possessed by a demon that torments her severely."
> —Matthew 15:22

> Then Jesus rebuked the demon in the boy, and it left him. From that moment the boy was well. —Matthew 17:18

> That evening after sunset, many sick and demon-possessed people were brought to Jesus. The whole town gathered at the door to watch. So Jesus healed many people who

were sick with various diseases, and he cast out many demons. But because the demons knew who he was, he did not allow them to speak.   — Mark 1:32-34

As you read these passages of Scripture, it's easy to say, "Wow! There was a lot of demon activity going on in Jesus's day!"

Indeed, there was. However, there are just as many demons today as in Jesus's day, and they are just as active. So you might ask, "Why then don't we see a lot of demon-possessed people today?"

I think we do, but we just don't recognize it. If you know how to look for it, you can practically see it everywhere. It's rampant. And it's getting worse. The one difference between the often-told stories of Jesus casting out demons and the lack of it today is simply because we're NOT Jesus! As the Son of God, demons cried out in absolute fear of Him!

In Jesus's day, the demons often screamed in fear as He approached the person whom they possessed. What's surprising is the number of people who were demon possessed. As the demons came face to face with the almighty Son of God (the One who created them), it frightened them because they knew who He was. They recognized Him as their Creator and God's Son.

Many were possessed by demons; and the demons came out at his command, shouting, "You are the Son of God!"   — Luke 4:41

I believe that's why we see so many demon possessions in the Bible. The fact is, demons have been constantly active since the day of Adam. They never get tired. As spirits, they are not subject to physical exhaustion. Plus, they've enjoyed thousands of years in dealing with mankind to hone their craft and use whatever devices they can to oppress you with anger, bitterness, depression, hatred, and the like — or even possess you.

While demons can "oppress" believers in Christ, they cannot "possess" believers in Jesus Christ. Why? See what the Word of God says:

> Don't you realize that your body is the temple of the Holy Spirit, who lives in you and was given to you by God? You do not belong to yourself, for God bought you with a high price.   — 1 Corinthians 6:19-20

God's Holy Spirit indwells every believer. No demon can kick Him out!

Demons need to possess people.

Jesus gave us some great insight into how demons work and what they need.

Notice in the verse below how Jesus refers to a person who was once demon possessed. He doesn't tell us how or why the demon left. But after the demon had left the individual, he wandered in dry places in search of another being to attach to. When the demon could not find one, he chose to reenter the original person, but with one caveat: to bring in seven additional demons more wicked than him. Read below:

> When an evil spirit leaves a person, it goes into the desert, seeking rest but finding

none. Then it says, "I will return to the person I came from." So it returns and finds its former home empty, swept, and in order. Then the spirit finds seven other spirits even more evil than itself, and they all enter the person and live there. And so that person is worse off than before. — Matthew 12:43-45

This information from Jesus would explain why the demons in Matthew chapter 8 begged Jesus to allow them to enter into a nearby herd of pigs after being cast out of two men who were guarding the pigs.

When Jesus arrived on the other side of the lake, in the region of the Gadarenes, two men who were possessed by demons met him. They lived in a cemetery and were so violent that no one could go through that area. They began screaming at him, "Why are you interfering with us, Son of God? Have you come here to torture us before God's appointed time?" There happened to be a large herd of pigs feeding in the distance. So the demons begged, "If you cast us out, send us into that herd of pigs." "All right, go!" Jesus commanded them. So the demons came out of the men and entered the pigs, and the whole herd plunged down the steep hillside into the lake and drowned in the water.

— Matthew 8:28-32

Demons vary in wickedness.

Just in case you missed it, Jesus gives us insight to a fundamental fact: Demons exist with varying levels of wickedness. Once again, read Matthew 12:43-45:

> When an evil spirit leaves a person, it goes into the desert, seeking rest but finding none. Then it says, "I will return to the person I came from." So it returns and finds its former home empty, swept and in order. Then the spirit finds seven other spirits even more evil than itself, and they all enter the person and live there. And so that person is worse off than before.

Demons look for leaders and influencers.

Evil forces are busy at work in this world—not only in your life, but especially in the lives of leaders and influencers. Evil tends to concentrate upon these leaders because of the impact they have on the lives of billions of people.

There's an old saying, "If you want to kill a snake, you have to cut off the head." Satan knows this. All leaders of people have tremendous influence over the lives they lead.

Satan and his minions aren't stupid. They're extremely intelligent. They understand man's vulnerabilities more than man does. Satan tried to destroy a man who had tremendous influence in his day. His name was Job. Here's the story:

> One day the members of the heavenly court came to present themselves before

the LORD, and the Accuser, Satan, came with them. "Where have you come from?" the LORD asked Satan. Satan answered the LORD, "I have been patrolling the earth, watching everything that's going on." Then the LORD asked Satan, "Have you noticed my servant Job? He is the finest man in all the earth. He is blameless—a man of complete integrity. He fears God and stays away from evil."

Satan replied to the LORD, "Yes, but Job has good reason to fear God. You have always put a wall of protection around him and his home and his property. You have made him prosper in everything he does. Look how rich he is! But reach out and take away everything he has, and he will surely curse you to your face!"

"All right, you may test him," the LORD said to Satan. "Do whatever you want with everything he possesses, but don't harm him physically." So Satan left the LORD's presence.

—Job 1:6-12

Notice how Satan confronts God about man's weakness. "Take away everything he has," he declares, "and he will surely curse you to your face!" He tried to take advantage of man's vulnerability to produce the response he wanted. It didn't work, though. In the end, Job endured Satan's relentless attacks. God blessed Job by giving him a double portion of everything Satan took from him.

Over the past 120 years, can you see how Satan and his demons have influenced world leaders?

While modern psychology would like to dismiss any evidence of the existence of demonic spirits, it cannot explain the carnage that men like Adolf Hitler, Josef Stalin, and Mao Tse-tung have committed during their sordid reigns of power.

It's hard for me to imagine that some psychopathic human action alone can perpetrate this magnitude of evil. As the Bible shows us, something far more intelligent, sinister, and cunning is at work. This type of evil has an intense hatred for both mankind and God. I don't believe even predatory animal species—especially among mammals—has such a wanton desire for carnage toward each other.

The twentieth century was the bloodiest century in the history of mankind. Approximately 8.5 *million* deaths happened in WWI, and another 61 *million* in WWII. That's not even counting the two worst holocausts that Russia's Joseph Stalin (1879-1953) and China's Mao Tse-tung (1893-1976) committed.

Joseph Stalin purged 60 million people who resisted him, and Mao Tse-tung killed about 60 million. Combined, these two communist dictators killed 120 million of their own citizens. That's more than the number of people who died in WWI and WWII *combined*. Added together, the total is a staggering 190 *million* people who died in the twentieth century. That's not even counting the other wars of this century.

A burning question most people are asking is "why?"

Modern science and psychology have tried to dismiss the idea of demons. However, small groups within their ranks are now admitting to evidence of malevolent forces that can supplant the human personality. There seems to be no other rational explanation for such behavior.

Someone once asked me, "Do you think Adolf Hitler was demon possessed?" I answered with a resounding, "Yes!" In fact, I believe Satan personally was involved in this man's life—just as he was in the life of Judas Iscariot, who betrayed Jesus for thirty pieces of silver.

Hitler's aide, Hermann Rauschning, even told in his book *Hitler Speaks* how Hitler would enter trances when he spoke at various political rallies. Hermann described Hitler as a medium for spirits — spirits that would possess him.

He added,

> One cannot help thinking of him as a medium. For most of the time, mediums are ordinary, insignificant people. Suddenly, they are endowed with what seems to be supernatural powers, which sets them apart from the rest of humanity. The medium is possessed. Once the crisis is passed, they fall back again into mediocrity. It was in this way, beyond any doubt, that Hitler was possessed by forces outside of himself— almost demonical forces of which the individual man Hitler was only a temporary vehicle. The mixture of the banal and the supernatural created that insupportable duality of which power was conscious in his presence … It was like looking at a bizarre face whose expression seemed to reflect an unbalanced state of mind coupled with a disquieting impression of hidden powers.

Rauschning went on to say how Hitler admitted he suffered many terrible nightmares. He spoke of how Hitler would wake up screaming in terror speaking about spirits. Hitler also told him he saw a "new man" in his dreams. *"He is intrepid and cruel. I was afraid of him."*

Trevor Ravenscroft's book *Spear of Destiny* says of Hitler, "Rauschning himself knew only too well that Hitler had abandoned himself to forces, which were carrying him away—forces of dark and destructive violence!"

The same was true with Stalin. After Lenin died, he ruled Soviet Russia from 1924 to 1953. He was responsible for the deaths of 60 million people during the Communist purge, a most horrific event. A mere human is not capable of such carnage. Most people agree there were demonic forces controlling him. Only preternatural spirits show such evil disdain and callousness for the human race.

Many associates and relatives of Stalin confirm this same mindset in their writings about him. Stalin's daughter Svetlana Alliluyeva said a terrible demon had possessed Stalin. She wrote, "Beria [the Soviet minister of interior] seemed to have had a diabolic link with all our family ... Beria was a frightening, wicked demon ... A terrible demon had taken possession of my father's soul."

How a demon gets a stronghold in your life.

A spiritual war is raging all around you. The apostle Paul reminds us in 2 Corinthians of the following:

For though we walk in the flesh, we do not war according to the flesh.

—2 Corinthians 10:4

You may feel like you're battling someone at work, but ask yourself, "What's really behind all the infighting?" You may feel like you're battling your spouse, but ask yourself, "What's really stirring the pot of anger, bitterness, and frustration in my marriage?"

Every day, you battle several things:

- your own sinful nature
- the sinful nature of others
- demonic influences

Life isn't easy. God never told us it would be. Nevertheless, He does give us instructions on how to make it better and how to find genuine peace and joy in life—something the world and demons can't offer.

Before we discuss the ways we can defeat demonic activity and influences, let's take a look at how they start.

First, realize you were born with a sinful nature just like every other human being since Adam and Eve sinned against God in the Garden of Eden. At conception, you inherited the sinful nature of your parents. Due to that original sin, the seeds of sin have been sown into the human race and it's natural for all of us to sin.

What is sin? Anything that goes against God's holy will.

Secondly, realize that demons love it when you sin. They enjoy any rebellious attitude you

might have toward God. In fact, they work hard
to convince you to turn your heart against God
and the truth of how He feels about you. Instead
of knowing how much He loves you, they want
you to be convinced that He hates you. Instead of
realizing how important you are to God, they want
you to feel that God doesn't care about you at all.
Instead of realizing how the challenges in life are
God's way of bringing you to Him and the life He
wants you to have, demons will try to convince
you that God is punishing you. Your mind is the
battleground. Either you'll believe the Bible and
what God says in it, or you'll believe what the
demons and the demonic influences of the world
say about God.

When you realize this, it's the first step to finding
victory over the evil spirits that try to rob you of the
joy and inner peace God wants you to have.

Thirdly, since your mind is the battleground,
you must learn how to bring every thought into a
proper perspective. Our weapons against demonic
spirits are not earthly weapons—such as a gun or
knife. The Bible says our weapons are spiritual
weapons. The three most powerful weapons you
can have against demonic activity are 1) a good
knowledge of the Bible, 2) prayer, and 3) faith in
the fact that all demons are under the authority of
Jesus Christ. Notice the passage below:

For the weapons of our warfare are not
carnal but mighty in God for pulling down
strongholds, casting down arguments and
every high thing that exalts itself against the

knowledge of God, bringing every thought
into captivity to the obedience of Christ.
—2 Corinthians 10:4-5

Demons begin with your mind, telling you
things that can stir your emotions.

They start playing mind games with you.
Then those become emotional games. If you allow
these things to continue, sooner or later terrible
emotional feelings and negative thinking will
prevail over you.

Let me share an example of what I mean.

I've lain in bed several nights thinking about
conversations I've had with someone who made
me angry. These thoughts would fester for hours as
I thought, "Why didn't I say this or that?" I tossed
and turned over these thoughts. Sometimes I even
sweated over them. At times I've even jumped out
of bed and stormed through the house thinking,
"How could I have been so stupid to let them say
that to me?"

Has that ever happened to you?

Here's what happens. First, your sinful nature
gets the best of you. Secondly, when your sinful
nature takes over it becomes fertile soil for evil
spirits to offer further suggestions. As you dwell
on it even more, you become emotionally charged
with adrenaline coursing through your veins until
you're deeply troubled in mind and heart.

My solution to those encounters is God. After
several hours of stewing in anger, God will often
interrupt me and remind me to simply give the
situation over to Him. Only when I do that do I
find peace.

Evil spirits work hard to create strongholds in our lives. A stronghold is anything that has a grip on you. It controls you. The Bible says strongholds come from one of three issues: the lust of the eyes, a love of money and things, and the pride of life.

> For the world offers only a craving for physical pleasure, a craving for everything we see, and pride in our achievements and possessions. These are not from the Father, but are from this world.   —1 John 2:16

Eventually a stronghold manifests itself in an addiction to work, alcohol, drugs, pornography, illicit sex, adultery, lying, hatred, bitterness, or anything else that is in direct contrast to what God wants for you.

Fortunately there's an antidote for that. God wants you to know you can conquer these strongholds and demonic influences in your life. That's what the next chapter is all about. It will show you how to be set free!

Chapter 9

Defeating Evil Spirits

L et me start with one profound truth. There's only one way to find real peace, real freedom, and real protection from the schemes of the devil and the minions that blindly follow him. That's Jesus Christ. When you decide to give your life to Him as your Lord and Savior, you'll find genuine love, peace, purpose, power, and protection that surpass all understanding.

This truth is probably no better illustrated than in the story told in Acts 19. Luke records the story, demonstrating how powerless people are against demons without Christ. If you've never accepted Jesus Christ into your life, you really have zero personal power to control your sinful nature or conquer evil spirits.

While you read the story below, remember that the men who practiced exorcism in this particular story were religious men. They were the sons of one of Israel's leading priests. While they were religious, they did not have a personal relationship with Jesus Christ.

Here's a very important note: Demons aren't impressed or influenced by religious people. They are only affected by Jesus Christ, their Creator. The reason they respond to the command of a believer in Christ is simple—it's the power granted to us by Jesus Christ and the use of His name.

God gave Paul the power to perform unusual miracles. When handkerchiefs or aprons that had merely touched his skin were placed on sick people, they were healed of their diseases, and evil spirits were expelled. A group of Jews was traveling from town to town casting out evil spirits. They tried to use the name of the Lord Jesus in their incantation, saying, "I command you in the name of Jesus, whom Paul preaches, to come out!" Seven sons of Sceva, a leading priest, were doing this. But one time when they tried it, the evil spirit replied, "I know Jesus, and I know Paul, but who are you?" Then the man with the evil spirit leaped on them, overpowered them, and attacked them with such violence that they fled from the house, naked and battered. The story of what happened spread quickly all through Ephesus, to Jews and Greeks alike. A solemn fear descended on the city, and the name of the Lord Jesus was greatly honored. Many who became believers confessed their sinful practices. A number of them who had been practicing sorcery brought their incantation books and burned them at a public bonfire. The value

of the books was several million dollars. So
the message about the Lord spread widely
and had a powerful effect. — Acts 19:11-20

Demonic activity is all around you, and it's
important to take this statement very seriously.
Demons fear Jesus, and they fear those who are
His. They recognize those of us who are believers
because we are filled with God's Holy Spirit when
we receive Christ into our lives. They have spiritual
eyes and can see those who are possessed by the
Holy Spirit of God and those who aren't.

I don't mean to scare you, but demons can do
strange things.

In Genesis 6, the Bible teaches how several of
them became sexually involved with women. As a
result, many giants were born in the land. From this
arose stories about Greek mythical mini-gods such
as Hercules, Hades, Zeus, and the like.

How to Defeat Demonic Activity That's
Happening Around You

Why was Jesus so effective in banishing demons,
causing them to scream in anguish and flee from
His presence? Because He was (and is) God in the
flesh. The Bible says demons tremble at the name
and thought of Jesus (James 2:19). They know they
are absolutely powerless before Him. They also
know He will one day throw them into the Lake
of Fire that was prepared for Satan and the angels
who followed him. That's why the terrified demons
asked Jesus at least twice when He expelled them
from a person who was possessed:

Have you come to destroy us?
                    —Mark 1:24; Luke 4:34

Jesus said, "Greater is He that is in you, than he that is in the world." Here is Jesus's promise to all of us who have accepted Him into our lives: He is greater in power than anything Satan can throw at us. That's also why Paul had such authority over demons.

The sad part of the story we just read is that the seven sons of Sceva never understood this. They only saw how Paul could cast out demons in the name of Jesus. Seeing how the demons fled in great numbers, these seven sons decided to bring fame to themselves through exorcism. They got the proverbial cart before the horse. They didn't realize the power to cast out demons came from the Holy Spirit who indwells believers in Jesus. Having Jesus as your Lord and Savior makes all the difference in the world, especially when both the physical demands of nature and the spiritual forces that surround us all work to affect our lives in more ways than we can imagine.

After the apostle Paul revealed the real powers behind the scenes, he also told us how to take control of these powers.

> Stand therefore, having girded your waist with truth, having put on the breastplate of righteousness, and having shod your feet with the preparation of the gospel of peace; above all, taking the shield of faith with which you will be able to quench all the fiery darts of the wicked one. And take the helmet of salvation, and the sword of the

Spirit, which is the word of God; praying always with all prayer and supplication in the Spirit, being watchful to this end with all perseverance and supplication for all the saints.   —Ephesians 6:13-16 NKJV

It's important to know that Satan and his demonic forces tremble at God's power! They were kicked out of heaven. They are extremely limited in their capacity. According to the Bible, man was created a little lower than the angels; therefore, if we're a little lower than the angels, then they are only a little higher than us. The disparity between God's power to protect you and their power to harm you is infinite. They are powerless—absolutely powerless—to exert any authority or action over you when you exercise the tools Paul describes above. Let me spell it out for you.

God's armor against demonic activity consists of six things:

1. **"Girded your waist with truth"** - There's only one truth, and that's God's Word, the Bible. You need to read it, study it, memorize it, and live it. In Matthew 4, Jesus convinced the devil to leave Him alone after throwing Scripture at him. Satan tried to throw Scripture back at Jesus, but with an evil twist. Fortunately, Jesus countered it with the Scripture of truth. You'll learn later that Satan knows the Bible very well. He's had thousands of years to study it, and he'll use it against you if you're not careful.
2. **"Breastplate of righteousness"** - That means you need to give your life to Christ so that

He can put His righteousness upon you and wash away your sins, allowing you to pray freely before God. It also refers to living the right kind of life—the kind of life God asks you to live.

3. **"Gospel of peace"** - God commands that we walk in peace with our fellow man. That's a sharp contrast to the false religions that plague the world calling for war, hatred, and the killing of those who don't comply.

4. **"Shield of faith"** - The way to block Satan's arrows fired at you is to use the shield of faith. That means having faith in God, in His power to protect you, and in His power to command His forces to interact and defend the onslaught of your adversary.

5. **"Helmet of salvation"** - Salvation is a term the Bible uses to mean saved from an eternal separation from God in a place called hell. Paul tells us that our head has to be protected by giving our whole life to the Lordship of Jesus Christ. And if Jesus is not Lord of all, chances are He's not Lord at all! To overcome evil, Jesus must be your Lord.

6. **"Sword of the Spirit"** - This is the Word of God, the Bible. God's Word tells us how to live a wonderful and joy-filled life. While God doesn't promise the absence of trials and deep pain, He offers Himself to carry our burden and our pain as well as His guidance and wisdom to help us endure trials and get to the other side. His Word provides all the answers we need to live by and to defend ourselves.

God never sugarcoats anything. He tells it straight up. He lets us know how to battle Satan and his demonic forces—and how to claim victory! Note what God says in the book of 1 Peter:

> Stay alert! Watch out for your great enemy, the devil. He prowls around like a roaring lion, looking for someone to devour.
>
> 1 Peter 5:8

Knowing that a battle is raging around you is winning half the battle.

Knowing how a loving God wants you to defend yourself and use His help to defeat Satan's attack on you and your family is winning the other half of the battle.

So win!

My Personal Encounter with Demons

Shortly after I started a church in my hometown of Lee's Summit, Missouri, our congregation started to grow. We initially met in the living room of our home with about five families. My wife, who is a fabulous decorator, was so gracious to move all the furniture out of the living room, pack it downstairs, and turn our living room into a roomful of plastic folding chairs.

After three months, we outgrew our living room and moved to a hotel conference area. Three months later, we needed to move again and found a church for sale that fit our price range. We purchased the building, its land, and a small house in the back part of the property.

It didn't start right away, but soon after we moved in I started to hear footsteps in the auditorium upstairs. My office was converted from a closet in the basement. While I studied the Bible and prepared for three messages each week, I would hear footsteps across the wooden floor above. Sometimes I would hear the front door open. Each time I heard these noises, I would run upstairs to see who it was. And each time, no one was there.

After about a month, I'd had enough! By this time I had ruled out the wind, the building creaking, and my imagination. These door openings and footsteps across the auditorium floor were becoming a daily activity and very unnerving. Finally I jumped from my office chair, stormed upstairs ready to charge hell with a squirt gun, and bolted into the auditorium. As I entered, I yelled, "Okay, demons. I know it's you! The game is up! I'm demanding you in the powerful name of Jesus, the Son of God, to stop this stuff right now! I command you to leave! I command you to leave and never come back to this place where we worship the name of Jesus, your Creator. Otherwise, I will ask Him to destroy you before your time!"

I was so mad!

From that moment on, I never heard the noises again.

Christians have nothing to fear. Satan and his demons are fearful of Jesus. They must flee at the command of His name.

Read the verses below and see how much demons fear Jesus:

As Jesus was climbing out of the boat, a man who was possessed by demons came out to meet him. For a long time, he had been homeless and naked, living in a cemetery outside the town. As soon as he saw Jesus, he shrieked and fell down in front of him. Then he screamed, "Why are you interfering with me, Jesus, Son of the Most-High God? Please, I beg you, don't torture me!" For Jesus had already commanded the evil spirit to come out of him. This spirit had often taken control of the man. Even when he was placed under guard and put in chains and shackles, he simply broke them and rushed out into the wilderness, completely under the demon's power. Jesus demanded, "What is your name?" "Legion," he replied, for he was filled with many demons. The demons kept begging Jesus not to send them into the bottomless pit.   —Luke 8:27-31

Once when he was in the synagogue, a man possessed by a demon—an evil spirit— began shouting at Jesus, "Go away! Why are you interfering with us, Jesus of Nazareth? Have you come to destroy us? I know who you are —the Holy One of God!"
                —Luke 4:33-34

Only true believers in Christ have the authority to command demons. If you're not a true follower of Christ, don't attempt to cast out demons. While demons fear the name of Jesus and tremble in horror at the thought of God, an unbeliever has no authority to use the name of Jesus—and the demons know it. Remember what happened to the seven sons of Sceva (Acts 19:13-16).

Listen, if you're a Christian, God has given you the right to command evil spirits in Jesus's name. As a joint-heir with Christ, you are under His authority. Consequently, they tremble in fear and must obey! Look at these two verses below:

> You say you have faith, for you believe that there is one God. Good for you! Even the demons believe this, and they tremble in terror. —James 2:19

> But don't rejoice because evil spirits obey you; rejoice because your names are registered in heaven. —Luke 10:20

There is one caveat, though. Some demons—or even groups of demons—are so powerful when they possess someone that it takes more than just commanding them in Jesus's name to defeat them. Here's what Jesus says:

> And when He had come into the house, His disciples asked Him privately, "Why could we not cast it out?" So He said to them, "This kind can come out by nothing but prayer and fasting." —Mark 9:28-29

Demons can even combine in number and form a very powerful group:

> For He said to him, "Come out of the man, unclean spirit!" Then He asked him, "What is your name?" And he answered, saying, "My name is Legion; for we are many." —Mark 5:8-9

A Documented Spirit on Spook Light Road

My next encounter with the spirit world occurred on the back roads south of Joplin, Missouri—just beyond the village of Hornet in an area known by locals as "The Devil's Promenade." I'll share more about this very unique encounter later in the book; however, this phenomenon is not unique in itself. It has captured a lot of media attention over the years, having been investigated by the Army Corps of Engineers in 1946 as well as featured on well-known TV news shows such as *20/20*. It's interesting to note the Army Corps of Engineers recorded it as a "mysterious light of unknown origin." Truthfully, there are things happening in this world that science just cannot explain.

I believe the Bible can!

Many people have tried to explain the strange light as anything from atmospheric gases to car headlights. While hundreds, and perhaps thousands, of people have experienced Spooklight, few have experienced this unique phenomenon in the way my friends and I did one night while turning onto Spooklight Road.

I had just attended a wedding ceremony in Joplin for a couple of coworkers. After the wedding, my friends Mike King, Jerry Powell, and Gordon Buboltz became inquisitive about going down to Spooklight Road. They asked me if I wanted to go, but I assured them it was a waste of time. I had been to Spooklight Road on a couple of occasions a few years before but never saw a thing. Even though there had been thousands of eyewitnesses and a personal story from my girlfriend's dad, who had a bizarre encounter with Spooklight when he was a teenager in Joplin, I still wasn't hopeful. Yet we all piled into Jerry's 1977 Malibu as I gave directions to Spooklight Road.

It was about ten o'clock that night as we approached Spooklight Road. Jerry drove while I sat shotgun. Mike and Gordon were in the back. As we approached, Mike said excitedly, "Man, wouldn't that be cool if we see it tonight?"

I reminded him of my failed encounters and warned him not to get his hopes up.

I told Jerry, "Okay, it's the next left. That's the beginning of Spooklight Road." Everyone was gripped with excitement except me—I'd lost all excitement on my last encounter.

The moment we turned left, we all started shouting. There it was! Right in front of us! Not one of us expected to see what we saw that night. It was a large light roughly five feet in diameter, slightly yellow but with no glow or radiance. It hovered about five feet above the middle of the road only twenty-five feet ahead of us. It seemed to be waiting for us to arrive.

Right away, Jerry stopped the car but kept the engine running. We stared at the light for several minutes, hardly believing what our eyes were beholding. It made no movement to get out of our way. It felt like it was staring at us just as much as we were staring at it.

From the back, Mike yelled to Jerry, "Let's get closer!"

Jerry released the brake and added some gas. We moved slowly toward the light. We got within about fifteen feet when it started to move away from us while maintaining its same height above the road. The light moved at the same speed we moved. Mike told Jerry to go a little faster—and he did, but not by much. The light began to pick up speed, putting more distance between us. We came to another stop, and it stopped immediately. We went nuts! We just couldn't believe what was happening.

This was no atmospheric gas or car light. This was something else that science could never explain. That's when we decided to do something bold. We decided to ram it with Jerry's car.

Mike, the most adventurous one of the four, yelled, "Ram it, Jerry!"

Jerry floored the pedal, and the gravel beneath the wheels flew behind us. As we approached the light, it began to take off. It flew up the hill in front of us at a much faster speed, still maintaining the same distance off the road. But now it moved from one side of the road to the other in an "s" maneuver. The faster we went, the faster the light moved. We could see it was really moving out. It would go over a hill, then down the hill, then up a hill, then down another hill—all the while maintaining the same height above the road and moving from side to side.

By the time we reached 45 mph on that hilly, gravel road, Spooklight flew even faster—at least 100 mph or more. In no time, it flew about one mile ahead of us before it vanished left around a corner.

What was this strange phenomenon that the Army Corps of Engineers could not explain? I believe it is a demonic spirit.

Why would I believe that?

First, God's holy angels serve to follow a specific command of God to function in the capacity of either providing a message or in protecting or guiding someone. Demons are not under those constraints. They like to promote fear.

This wandering spirit near Joplin, Missouri is an adrenaline junkies high. It serves no known Godly purpose. It promotes the paranormal and produces immediate fear.

The Bible tells us in 2 Timothy 1:7 – "For God has not given us a spirit of fear and timidity, but of power, love, and self-discipline."

God is not in the business of promoting fear: something Satan and his demons love to do. That's why God tells us to "test the spirits."

We are to test the spirits.

> Dear friends, do not believe everyone who claims to speak by the Spirit. You must test them to see if the spirit they have comes from God. For there are many false prophets in the world. This is how we know if they have the Spirit of God: If a person claiming to be a prophet acknowledges that Jesus Christ came in a real body, that person has the Spirit of God. But if someone claims to be a prophet and does not acknowledge the truth about Jesus, that person is not from God. Such a person has the spirit of the Antichrist, which you heard is coming into the world and indeed is already here.
>
> —1 John 4:1-3

What God, angels, and demons are doing

In the unseen spiritual world, God is sending His Holy Spirit to convict you and compel you to turn your life to Christ. The angels are doing everything they can to battle the demons that have lost themselves to eternal damnation. These demons are doing everything they can to take you with them. Demons will never have forgiveness. The moment they were deceived by Satan and followed him, they were doomed to eternal destruction in the Lake of Fire. For a demon, what do they have to lose if you go to Hell? All the more reason for them to convince you through pride, lust, power, money, status or anything to distract you and prevent you from giving your life to Christ. Their path leads to eternal destruction, and they want to take you with them.

When God created Hell, the Bible says He created it specifically for Satan and the wicked angels that followed him. But once sin was sown into the human race via Adam, there's nothing a loving God can do unless man accepts God's wonderful gift of His Son and eternal life. He loves you so much He's inviting you to join Him in Heaven by accepting His Son, Jesus Christ. But sin causes us to reject or simply ignore God's Son as His gift for eternal life. What can God do? He's given you free will. He never made you a robot. You have a choice! That's how much God loves you! What choice will you make?

Just because we can't see it, hear it, taste it, smell it or feel it doesn't mean it's not real. The spiritual world is very real. It's just as complex and active as our physical world is. It's filled with angels and demons fighting over us. The Bible tells us God's plan of reconciliation is perfect. He desires to bring every human being to a closer relationship with Jesus Christ and to assure eternal life with

Him. But Satan (whom we'll discuss later) rebelled against God due to his insatiable appetite to be like God. When God kicked him out of His presence along with the many thousands of angels (called demons) who defected and joined Satan's scheme, it started spiritual warfare. We're caught in the middle of that war.

Even though we all have a sinful nature (through the sinfulness of Adam, the first man) and natural desires of the heart filled with selfish ambitions, God sent His Son, Jesus Christ, to die on the cross as the perfect, sinless sacrifice for man's sin. And now, for all who will believe in Jesus Christ and seek forgiveness for their sins and turn to God, they have the opportunity to enjoy eternal life in Heaven in the presence of God His angels. But for those who reject Jesus Christ and the forgiveness He offers, the stain of sin will keep them from entering into the presence of God and enjoying Him forever. Those who reject God's Son, Jesus Christ, will be carried by the angels into Hell and eventually the Lake of Fire (which I'll discuss later). Not because God is a mean God and wants us to suffer, but because God has given each of us free will to choose to accept Christ or reject Him. Each of us has that choice. What will be your decision? What eternal destination do you want?

What about ghosts and visiting spirits?

As a kid, I remember growing up watching the hit cartoon, "Casper, The Friendly Ghost." I loved Casper. Unlike all the others, he was the friendly ghost.

Ghosts are often considered deceased human beings whose spirit still roams the Earth with unfinished business or revenge. But that can't be. Human spirits don't roam the Earth according to the Bible. They are carried by angels into either Heaven or Hell, and are confined there. They don't have the ability to reappear on Earth of their own volition. Only God can give them the power to do so.

The only time we see the spirit of someone coming back to Earth in the Bible, though, was Saul, King of Israel. He used a witch to summon the spirit of Samuel, the old prophet. When Samuel came forth, the witch was scared to death, and Samuel was very angry with Saul. In fact, God commands us not to summon the spirits of the deceased. That's dabbling in the occult.

Like you, I've watched popular TV shows countless times that feature a spirit medium or psychic medium. These shows have astounded us with the medium's ability to convey messages from the spirit world. I don't know about all of them, but I do believe some of them may be very real. Why? These psychic mediums aren't receiving messages from a loved one like they say they are. No, they're deluding us to thinking they are. They aren't. The Bible says so.

You must remember, Satan and his host of demons have honed their craft for thousands of years. They are very subtle. They know your loved ones. They can use a psychic medium to convey messages of love and hope by providing information only you and your loved one know. But, know this, your loved one is not communicating with you. The psychic is dabbling in the occult. That can be very dangerous, both for the psychic and you.

The Bible warns us about this:

> For such are false apostles, deceitful workers,
> transforming themselves into apostles of
> Christ. And no wonder! For Satan himself
> transforms himself into an angel of light.
> Therefore, it is no great thing if his ministers
> also transform themselves into ministers of
> righteousness, whose end will be according
> to their works.   — 2 Corinthians 11:13-14

I know this may hurt, but would you rather know the truth or believe a lie? That's why we have God's Word so we can discern what the truth is.

But what if you've actually seen the image of a loved one?

Well, I believe you may have seen just that – an image generated by a spirit. It could have either been an angel of God or a demon spirit.

I have family members who are great Christians who have seen their spouse or father or mother and truly believed they were in the room with them. I don't doubt that at all. However, the Bible is very clear about this. The spirits of the deceased cannot roam this world.

So what could that image represent? In many cases, I believe God may have allowed an angel to appear in the form of that loved one. I believe God would do that as an act of His love for that person to help strengthen them and provide hope, encouragement, love, security and whatever else that person may need. Remember, God loves you so much and will do many things to show His love to you. He will even allow His angels to materialize and take the form of a human being as we've often seen in Scripture. I believe God allowed an angel to serve and minister to that person to bring to him or her comfort. God loves His children and does many things to encourage them and love them.

If you feel like you're being attacked by evil spirits in some way, please let us pray with you. Visit my book's website at **www.AngelsUTM.com** and let us know how we can help!

Chapter 10

Satan Doesn't Have a Pitchfork

I remember trick-or-treating when I was a kid. Back in the 1960s, we had some pretty cool outfits. I'll never forget one of them—a representation of Satan himself. The costume was made up of a dark red fabric combined with a red-faced mask and a three-pronged pitchfork. It looked pretty scary, even for a costume. But is this what the devil really looks like? And is he even real?

It's interesting to note only 27 percent of Christians in America believe Satan is real, according to a nationwide survey conducted by The Barna Group. The other 73 percent believe he's either a mere symbol of evil or just doesn't exist at all. All over the world, there are varied interpretations on the existence of Satan.

To a Muslim, he's the United States—the Great Satan. To others, Satan has horns, a tail, and carries a pitchfork. To still others, he represents the dark side of humanity.

According to a self-proclaimed Satanist David R. Ondrejko (aka VonDraco), "What I believe in is a Satan that represents the so-called 'dark side' of humanity. He represents selfishness, anger, lust, hatred, pride and all the allegedly negative emotions. He represents getting whatever you want. He is not real, in the sense that you and I are real. What he represents is real. Satan is as real as I am. What I mean by this is that insofar as I manifest the Satanic ethos, Satan becomes real through me. I am, at my best (worst?), the incarnation of Satan Himself. What is the Satanic ethos? At its simplest, it is pure egoism; total and exclusive concern for myself."

Regardless of what people think, however, the Bible gives us a different viewpoint. Throughout its pages, you'll find a real being who orchestrates all the evil rampant in the world. If fact, there's plenty of biblical evidence that Satan is a real person.

Seven Old Testament books teach that Satan is a real being (Genesis, 1 Chronicles, Job, Psalms, Isaiah, Ezekiel, and Zechariah). Every New Testament writer who mentions Satan refers to him as a real person.

In the Gospel of Matthew, Jesus portrays the devil as a real person. Jesus sees him, speaks with him, and is tempted by him. Eventually Satan is defeated by Jesus and physically leaves him.

Then Jesus was led by the Spirit into the wilderness to be tempted there by the devil. For forty days and forty nights he fasted and became very hungry. During that time the devil came and said to him, "If you are the Son of God, tell these stones to become loaves of bread." But Jesus told him, "No! The Scriptures say, People do not live by bread alone, but by every word that comes from the mouth of God." Then the devil took him to the holy city, Jerusalem, to the highest point of the Temple, and said, "If you are the Son of God, jump off! For the Scriptures say, He will order his angels to protect you. And they will hold you up with their hands so you won't even hurt your foot on a stone." Jesus responded, "The Scriptures also say, You must not test the LORD your God." Next the devil took him to the peak of a very high mountain and showed him all the kingdoms of the world and their glory. "I will give it all to you," he said, "if you will kneel down and worship me." "Get out of here, Satan," Jesus told him. "For the Scriptures say, You must worship the LORD your God and serve only him." Then the devil went away, and angels came and took care of Jesus.

—Matthew 4:1-7

Many people believe in Jesus but sincerely question the idea of Satan as a real being. However, if you're a person who believes in Jesus, whether as a prophet of God or as the Son of God, you must believe in the reality of Satan as well. Jesus taught on several occasions that Satan is a real being. To believe Jesus to be a representative of God and of truth means you must accept His teaching about Satan and who and what he is.

Other writers such as Paul (Ephesians 6:10-12), John (1 John 3:8), James (James 4:7), and Peter (1 Peter 5:8) all describe Satan as a real person.

In addition to biblical evidence, there's also philosophical, experiential, and religious evidence that supports this fact as well.

Philosophically

Philosophical evidence supports the fact that nearly everyone around the world believes in a good-versus-bad concept.

Experientially

Satan worshippers will tell you he is a real being and can speak of his existence.

Religiously

Religious evidence supports the fact that all religions around the world believe in him or the essence of his nature.

Satan Goes by Many Names

In the Bible, the name Satan is mentioned fifty-two times and means "adversary." He is also called "the devil," meaning "the one who trips up," thirty-seven times. The following are some additional names given to him in the King James Bible:

- Isaiah 14 – "Lucifer"
- Ezekiel 28 – "the anointed cherub"
- Matthew 4 – "the tempter"
- Luke 11 – "Beelzebub, the chief of demons"
- John 8 – "the father of lies"
- John 16 – "the prince of this world"
- John 17 – "the evil one"

- Ephesians 2 – "prince of the power of the air"
- 2 Corinthians 4 – "god of this age"
- Revelation 12 – "old serpent"
- Revelation 12 – "the dragon"
- Revelation 12 – "the accuser of the brethren"

Who Exactly Is He?

1. A former cherub of God

If you refer back to our study of the cherubim, you'll have a good idea why Satan's heart could be lifted up in pride. He was absolutely stunning in every way. As a former cherub, he was positioned at the very feet of God. He served as one who worshipped Him and sang praises to Him. Let's look at Ezekiel 28 and see how God describes this unique being:

> You were the seal of perfection, full of wisdom and perfect in beauty. You were in Eden, the garden of God; every precious stone was your covering: The sardius, topaz, and diamond, beryl, onyx, and jasper, sapphire, turquoise, and emerald with gold. The workmanship of your timbrels and pipes was prepared for you on the day you were created. You were the anointed cherub who covers; I established you; you were on the holy mountain of God; you walked back and forth in the midst of fiery stones. You were perfect in your ways from the day you were created, till iniquity was found in you. By the abundance of your trading you became filled with violence within, and you sinned;

therefore, I cast you as a profane thing out of the mountain of God; and I destroyed you, O covering cherub, from the midst of the fiery stones. Your heart was lifted up because of your beauty; you corrupted your wisdom for the sake of your splendor; I cast you to the ground, I laid you before kings, that they might gaze at you. You defiled your sanctuaries by the multitude of your iniquities, by the iniquity of your trading; therefore, I brought fire from your midst; it devoured you, and I turned you to ashes upon the earth in the sight of all who saw you. All who knew you among the peoples are astonished at you; you have become a horror, and shall be no more forever.

— Ezekiel 28:12-19

While some people see this as a prophecy against the king of Tyre, it's more than that. By applying very simple Bible study rules to this passage, you'll easily see how the first ten verses of this chapter refer to the actual physical king of Tyre. But then God shifts the prophecy to the spirit behind the king of Tyre — Satan himself.

In this passage, God provides an accounting of what Satan really is, what he looked like before his fall, what caused his fall, and what he has been reduced to today.

Look at what he was:

- A model of perfection (until evil was found within him)
- Full of wisdom

- Perfect in beauty
- Created by God
- Ordained and anointed as a mighty cherub who guarded the throne
- A being with total access to God

Look at what caused his fall:

- His heart was lifted up with pride.
- His beauty was a stumbling block.
- He sought his own splendor and glory.
- He committed "sinful trading," which must refer to his encouraging other angels to sin.

Look at what he was reduced to:

- God stripped him of his beauty.
- God kicked him out of heaven, sending him to the dust of the earth.
- He was shamed in front of the entire heavenly host.
- He will have an end one day.

2. The enemy of man

Most Christians have a distorted view of Satan. Many see Satan as nothing more than a spirit constantly battling God in heaven, but the Bible doesn't teach that. Yes, there is a battle raging around you, but it's over you. You are the target of his attacks.

Satan already knows he's lost his battle with God. Not only was he kicked out of heaven at the time of his rebellion, he was also profoundly defeated when Jesus, God's Son, died on the cross and rose from the grave three days later. Now, being the defeated foe he is, Satan has turned his attention to man. There are no more battles to fight with God. Man is the archenemy of Satan now. The Bible delivers this warning:

> Be sober, be vigilant; because your adversary the devil walks about like a roaring lion, seeking whom he may devour.
> —1 Peter 5:8

Satan is our "adversary." He doesn't like us one bit. In fact, he hates us. His mission is to "destroy" each one of us. He will do whatever it takes to create adversity in our lives. If he can bring us to a place to commit suicide, he's won.

So why does he have such a hatred for us? It's simple. We are the objects of God's affection. Every day Satan witnesses God's wonderful grace and mercy in our lives. He sees God's love toward us. He sees God's forgiveness and His enormous patience for us when we sin.

Satan has never had that experience with God. The moment Satan desired to be worshipped like God, it was all over for him. The sin of pride cost him dearly. For Satan, there were no second chances, no forgiveness, no opportunity to repent and make things right.

God tells us in Luke 12:48: "For everyone to whom much is given, from him much will be required." Satan and the angels who rebelled were given much. They were given the opportunity to see God in all His fullness. They were given the rare privilege to experience all God has to offer. Man has never had that opportunity. We live by faith. We've never had the privilege to stand in God's presence and experience His majesty like Satan and the angels have. Because of this opportunity, God relinquished any future opportunity Satan or his angels would have for forgiveness.

Satan is more than just our adversary wanting to destroy us. He's also seeking ways to perpetuate lies about himself, about you, about others, and about God.

Once when Jesus was speaking to a crowd, He shared something about Satan He really wanted His listeners to know. As the religious leaders attacked Him verbally, He knew there was an evil spirit behind their accusations. Listen to how Jesus contrasts the difference between Him and His purpose and the purpose of Satan:

> The thief does not come except to steal, and to kill, and to destroy. I have come that they may have life, and that they may have it more abundantly.   —John 10:10

No one knows Satan better than Jesus. He created him. He saw his rebellion and kicked him out of heaven because of it. Notice how He summarizes the purposes of Satan with three words: steal, kill, and destroy.

If you let him, Satan will steal your joy, your love, your respect, and your relationship with God. He'll also do what he can to kill. He'll kill your marriage, your love of life, your hope in the future, your confidence in others, and every relationship you have.

His Downfall

Satan's downfall is one of the most tragic stories of the Bible. God created him as one of the most beautiful of all His creation—a cherub. God gave him the awesome privilege of worshipping immediately before His presence at the base of His throne. Satan had a front-row seat to the creation of the entire universe, witnessing all the power, majesty, and glory of the very God who created him.

Sadly, pride filled his heart. In the book of Isaiah, God calls him by the name He originally gave him, Lucifer, meaning "shining one" or "morning star." In this book, God explains the reason for his downfall. Look at what pride did to him!

> How you are fallen from heaven, O Lucifer, son of the morning! How you are cut down to the ground, you who weakened the nations! For you have said in your heart: "I will ascend into heaven, I will exalt my throne above the stars of God; I will also sit on the mount of the congregation on the farthest sides of the north; I will ascend above the heights of the clouds; I will be like the Most-High." Yet you shall be brought down to Sheol, to the lowest depths of the Pit.
> —Isaiah 14:12-15

Pride brought Satan to a point where he wanted to be like God. He started to believe his own press releases! He took himself too seriously. He noticed he was one of God's most privileged and beautiful creations. It got him to thinking, "Hey, I'm really something! I could be like God!"

Notice what Satan says above:

- I will ascend into heaven
- I will exalt my throne above the stars (angels) of God.
- I will sit on the mount of the congregation (on God's throne).
- I will ascend above the heights of the clouds.
- I will be like the Most-High.

In fact, God commanded his servant Ezekiel to prophesy against Satan (the evil spirit behind the wickedness of the king of Tyre) because he wanted to be a god.

Therefore, thus says the Lord God: "Because you have set your heart as the heart of a god..." —Ezekiel 28:6

That was it. Satan just had to be a god. He saw the adoration and praise that almighty God received and wanted that for himself too. Consequently, he was expelled from God's presence. Jesus described his fall like this:

And He said to them, "I saw Satan fall like lightning from heaven." —Luke 10:18

God cast him to the earth to be the prince of this earth and the prince of the power of the air.

So the great dragon was cast out, that serpent of old, called the Devil and Satan, who deceives the whole world; he was cast

to the earth, and his angels were cast out
with him.   —Revelation 12:9

Although he wanted to be like God, the truth is
he is *nothing* like Him. Let me share with you what
the Bible tells us that Satan is NOT.

What Satan is NOT:

1. He is not self-existent.

Satan was created by God. Satan does not have
an eternal past like God. There was a definite point
in time when he was created. Note what the Bible
says:

> You were in Eden, the garden of God. Your
> clothing was adorned with every precious
> stone...all beautifully crafted for you and set
> in the finest gold. They were given to you on
> the day you were created.   —Ezekiel 28:13

2. He is not all-powerful.

Satan is jealous of God's power and wanted to
be worshipped like Him. The
reality about Satan that few people realize is just
how limited his powers and abilities are.
Most people don't realize Satan must appear
before God and give account of himself from time to
time. Although God is constantly aware of all Satan
is doing, He still requires Satan to come before His
presence occasionally and give account of his activities in the world. We see Satan coming before God
to give account of his actions on two separate occasions in the book of Job:

Now there was a day when the sons of God
came to present themselves before the LORD,
and Satan also came among them. And the
LORD said to Satan, "From where do you
come?" So Satan answered the LORD and
said, "From going to and fro on the earth,
and from walking back and forth on it."
                                                    —Job 1:6-7

Again there was a day when the sons of God
came to present themselves before the LORD,
and Satan came also among them to present
himself before the LORD. And the LORD said
to Satan, "From where do you come?" Satan
answered the LORD and said, "From going to
and fro on the earth, and from walking back
and forth on it."   —Job 2:1-2

If Satan were all-powerful, he wouldn't feel
the need to answer to God for his actions. Plus, he
wouldn't subject himself to God's authority.

In the first two chapters of the book of Job, God
praises Job as a wonderful servant. Satan challenges God, wanting to prove Him wrong. Would
Job still be a wonderful servant if he suffered
unprecedented personal attacks, deaths in his
family, destruction of his wealth, and the worst of
all assaults on his health? Satan was convinced Job
would curse God. But did he? Notice the supreme
power and authority God has over Satan's actions
and just how limited Satan is to God's command:

So Satan answered the LORD and said,
"Does Job fear God for nothing? Have You
not made a hedge around him, around his

household, and around all that he has on
every side? You have blessed the work of his
hands, and his possessions have increased
in the land. But now, stretch out Your hand
and touch all that he has, and he will surely
curse You to Your face!" And the Lord
said to Satan, "Behold, all that he has is in
your power; only do not lay a hand on his
person." So Satan went out from the presence of the Lord.   —Job 1:9-12

Notice again during the second time Satan
stands before God to give account of himself that
God brags on his servant Job. Satan once again
challenges God about the nature of man and
believes that if he could strip Job of his health, then
he would curse God to His face. However, God
knows the heart of Job and how Job will ultimately
respond. God allows Satan to attack Job's health but
commands Satan to spare his life. Satan obeys God
and is limited by God's command. Nevertheless, as
always God was right about his servant Job, and
Job passed this tough test:

So Satan answered the Lord and said, "Skin
for skin! Yes, all that a man has he will give
for his life. But stretch out Your hand now,
and touch his bone and his flesh, and he will
surely curse You to Your face!" And the Lord
said to Satan, "Behold, he is in your hand,
but spare his life." So Satan went out from
the presence of the Lord, and struck Job with
painful boils from the sole of his foot to the
crown of his head.   —Job 2:4-7

As you read the horrible attacks Job had to endure from Satan, it may make you wonder. Was God a little mean to allow Satan to attack such a righteous man? It certainly appears that way from a human perspective. But keep in mind that God will never allow you to be tested more than you're able to bear. God knew how things would turn out with Job. The Christian life is full of trials, but God uses those trials to test our faith, grow us, and demonstrate important aspects of His character we've never experienced. When Satan attacks, God never allows him to do anything to you that He knows you can't beat. It's up to you to choose to win the battle and receive His blessings in the end.

3. He is not all-knowing.

Satan only knows what God has disclosed to him. He's limited in his knowledge of future events. While some people think he can read our minds, he cannot! He does not have that ability. Only God knows our thoughts.

However, Satan can predict our behavior. As you read the previous verses about Job, you can see that Satan knows how man will react if prompted. He's had several thousand years to study man, and he knows how man responds to certain situations. In Job's case, Satan didn't know the heart and mind of Job. In spite of hurling every horrible thing at him, Job still retained his integrity with God.

4. He is not everywhere-present.

God is omnipresent; Satan is not. God doesn't need to walk to and fro across the earth to see what's going on, but Satan does. Using the previous verses in Job, see what Satan says about himself when God asked him what he was doing:

> So Satan answered the LORD and said, "From going to and fro on the earth, and from walking back and forth on it."
>
> —Job 1:6-7; Job 2:1-2

In essence, Satan isn't anything like God. While many people visualize a "God-like" persona of Satan, he is not. He's just a created being who is absolutely powerless before an all-powerful God. Satan doesn't have any of the same qualities as God. Satan is limited in knowledge, limited in ability, limited in space, limited in time, and limited in freedom. He's completely subject to God's authority.

Keep in mind that God and Satan are not battling it out in heaven. Yes, God's angelic forces and Satan's demonic forces are waging a war, but Satan knows he's defeated. The war is not against each other, but rather against you.

Chapter 11

The Covert Strategies of Evil

Satan doesn't want to be recognized. He desires to stay in the background. He couldn't care less if people worship him or not. Worship is not his focus. Your relationship to God is the only thing that matters to him. His anger is toward the object of God's affection. He knows the best way to get revenge is to steal people from God and destroy any relationship they might have with him.

Satan works covertly in a number of ways. I'd like to share those with you so you won't be ignorant of his evil schemes. The apostle Paul said:

> ...so that Satan will not outsmart us. For we are familiar with his evil schemes.
> —2 Corinthians 2:11

Half the battle is knowing how the enemy works and what kind of arsenal he uses.

Satan's ultimate purpose

Satan's all-consuming desire is to get you to reject God. He already knows he's defeated. He knows God will cast him into the Lake of Fire one day. Satan knows the battle is over. Therefore, there's no need for him to battle it out with God. Instead, he's chosen to work indirectly against God by directing the full brunt of his attacks upon man. Turning man—any man—away from God is a victory for him.

Satan doesn't play games. He's hell-bent on his mission to deceive, control, lie to, and destroy man. Man is the object of God's great love, and that's why Satan seeks to destroy us. To Satan, that's the ultimate revenge. He seeks to turn us away from God and His promise of eternal life in heaven through His Son Jesus Christ. Think about it. In heaven, we'll experience the wonderful presence of the Lord that Satan will never again experience. If Satan doesn't get heaven, then he doesn't want you to have it either.

You've seen a situation like this in the movies. Satan takes hostages. Instead of turning his gun upon you to make you talk, he turns the gun on someone you love.

Satan's best shot at revenge against God is simple. He wants to make sure you never get the life God wants you to have. Satan doesn't want you to have the joy, love, peace, and hope that God gives. He wants you miserable, depressed, angry, negative, unforgiving, fearful, oppressed, untrusting, and sour about life.

In his effort to turn you away from God, Satan uses several tactics:

- He'll allow you to read the Bible, but he'll confuse you with it and make you think it's too hard to understand and irrelevant for today.
- He'll allow you to go to church and enjoy it, but he'll use something or someone (including the moral indiscretion of a pastor or priest) to make you untrusting toward church.
- He'll allow you to think you're a Christian, but he'll make sure you don't act like one.
- He'll allow you to be a good moral person, but he'll work hard to make sure you don't cross the line and give your life to Jesus Christ.

Satan is the father of lies. Listen to how Jesus describes him:

> You are of your father the devil, and the desires of your father you want to do. He was a murderer from the beginning, and does not stand in the truth, because there is no truth in him. When he speaks a lie, he speaks from his own resources, for he is a liar and the father of it.　　　—John 8:44

As a way to destroy us, Satan uses lies. He lies to us and uses his demonic forces to lie to us. Any lie will do. He wants you to believe lies about God, about you, about your spouse, about your children, about your coworkers, and about the teaching of Scripture. He destroys man through lies. His lies have one purpose: to draw us away from God and His Word and dampen our relationship with God.

Here are at least five covert schemes he often uses:

1. The lying scheme

Lie #1 – You can't trust God.

Satan doesn't want you to believe God, believe in God, or even accept the validity of the Bible. He doesn't want you to have anything to do with either of them. He is fully aware of how the Bible can transform your life and grant insight into a relationship with God. He will do everything he can to downplay its veracity and the importance of what God has to say. Notice how he duped Eve, the first woman, into downplaying and negating what God said:

> One day he asked the woman, "Did God really say you must not eat the fruit from any of the trees in the garden?" "Of course we may eat fruit from the trees in the garden," the woman replied. "It's only the fruit from the tree in the middle of the garden that we are not allowed to eat. God said, You must not eat it or even touch it; if you do, you will die." "You won't die!" the serpent replied to the woman. "God knows that your eyes will be opened as soon as you eat it, and you will be like God, knowing both good and evil."
> —Genesis 3:1-5

See how he lied to Eve? He told her, "You won't die!" In other words, "God lied to you, Eve! You're not going to die! The real reason why God doesn't want you to eat from this tree is because it will make you like Him, and He doesn't want that!"

Unfortunately for all mankind, Eve believed him.

Has Satan ever lied to you about God? Has he tried to convince you the Bible isn't relevant today? Has he ever caused you to have some kind of beef with God because you just didn't understand why He allowed certain things to happen that seemed unfair? Has he ever told you the Bible can't be trusted because it's way too complicated and controversial?

He's great at creating doubt. He does it all through lies.

Lie #2 – God is a self-centered tough guy.

I've heard this statement so many times. It comes straight from Satan. He invented it. Look at the rest of the story in Genesis 3:

> "You won't die!" the serpent replied to the woman. "God knows that your eyes will be opened as soon as you eat it, and you will be like God, knowing both good and evil."
> — Genesis 3:1-5

Can you see how Satan is making God look selfish?

I've heard many people say they believe God is selfish. Why? Because He seeks to be worshipped. They find God selfish and cruel because He allows the killing of innocent babies. They judge Him harshly for demanding our obedience.

Satan uses these and other statements to push us away from God and the truth about Him.

Lie #3 – God is nothing more than a psychological crutch for people.

What is Satan's biggest problem and most covert lie? Pride. Satan was kicked out of heaven because of his pride. It's also his number one way to keep people out of heaven. Pride is his most important tool.

Have you ever heard somebody say, "We don't take charity!" Well, that strikes at the heart of pride. People are prideful. They want to make it on their own. They're self-sufficient, and they're proud of it. Essentially, there's nothing wrong with that to some extent. However, some people allow it to go too far.

I know several men who say they don't need God. They're the same men who tend to be self-sufficient, accusing Christians of using God as a psychological crutch. These men are fools, but they haven't recognized it yet. They're drowning in a world of self-created lies. They can't even see the handiwork of God all around us, and they refuse to cater to any need of God.

That's pride at its best, and Satan is proud of men who fall into that pit.

Once again, look at these verses in the book of Job and notice how Satan argues with God by understanding the sinful pride of man:

Satan replied to the LORD, "Yes, but Job has good reason to fear God. You have always put a wall of protection around him and his home and his property. You have made him prosper in everything he does. Look how rich he is! But reach out and take away everything he has, and he will surely curse you to your face!" —Job 1:9-11

Lie #4 – God doesn't care about you.

In one of the most incredible stories of the Bible, God used a man named Gideon and 300 men to destroy an army of more than 180,000 troops. It's the stuff great movies are made of. But here's one thing many people don't know. Gideon was mad at God.

While hiding his crop in a winepress, Gideon received a visit from the Lord. Because life was rough for the Israelites, who were living in fear for their lives, Gideon chose to vent his anger toward God. With all this tragedy, where was God? That's what Gideon wanted to know. Here's what he told the angel of the Lord:

"Sir," Gideon replied, "if the LORD is with us, why has all this happened to us? And where are all the miracles our ancestors told us about? Didn't they say the LORD brought us up out of Egypt? But now the LORD has abandoned us and handed us over to the Midianites." —Judges 6:13

Gideon just didn't feel the love! Rather than recognize all the sins the Israelites were committing, he chose to focus upon the devastation God allowed. He didn't care "why" things weren't working out for Israel. He was more intent on blaming God for the horrible things going on. In other words, he blamed God for not caring. Despite all this, God still came to Gideon and used 300 ordinary men to destroy an army of more than 180,000. That's a reminder of God's love for His people.

Has Satan ever raised doubts about God's love for you? Has he ever caused you to wonder whether God even cares for you at all? The truth is, God does care! Look at what Jesus said:

> And if God cares so wonderfully for flowers that are here today and thrown into the fire tomorrow, he will certainly care for you.
> —Luke 12:28

> Give all your worries and cares to God, for he cares about you. —1 Peter 5:7

Lie #5 – You aren't worthy of God.

Because you mean so much to God, Satan will do everything he can to make you feel the absolute opposite. Since God sees you as significant in His eyes, Satan will use whatever or whomever he can to make you feel insignificant. Since God considers you so worthy He would sacrifice His only Son on the cross, Satan will use others to make you feel unworthy. Since you're precious to God, Satan will do everything he can to make you feel like a mistake and a problem that needs to go away.

When God came to His servant Gideon, He addressed Gideon in a way Gideon never saw himself. See what the Lord said as he approached Gideon:

When the angle of the L<small>ORD</small> appeared to Gideon, he said, "The L<small>ORD</small> is with you, mighty warrior." —Judges 6:12

God called Gideon a "mighty warrior." No one was more surprised than Gideon. After all, he had never been in a war. He had never fought anyone. By his own admission, Gideon replied:

"Pardon me, my Lord, but how can I save Israel? My clan is the weakest in Manasseh, and I am the least in my family." —Judges 6:15

Gideon suffered from a poor self-image. But God saw something completely opposite. God called him a mighty warrior. Why? Because God sees us for who we can be with His help!

That's why the apostle Paul wrote:

I can do all things through Christ who strengthens me. —Philippians 4:13

To God, you are somebody! To God, you are important and worthy! However, Satan will do whatever he can to make you think differently. Don't listen to him!

Here's the advice the Bible gives when you feel Satan's attack upon you:

Therefore submit to God. Resist the devil and he will flee from you. —James 4:7

2. The "Don't worry...everyone's going to heaven" scheme

If I were Satan, this would be my biggest tool in the toolbox—making people assume they're going to heaven. Look, Satan doesn't want *anyone* going to heaven. He's the ultimate self-centered being. If he isn't going to be there, then why should anyone else?

Do you know anybody like that? If they can't have it, then you can't have it either?

Have you heard the rumors that there are many ways to get to God? That most everyone will spend eternity with God? That a loving God would never send anyone to hell? These are nothing more than false rumors spread by Satan. These lies prevent so many people from finding the truth about the requirements Jesus gave about having eternal life.

By His own admission, Jesus stated that most people will *NOT* make it to heaven. Listen to His riveting statement:

> You can enter God's Kingdom only through the narrow gate. The highway to hell is broad, and its gate is wide for the many who choose that way. But the gateway to life is very narrow and the road is difficult, and only a few ever find it.   —Matthew 7:13-14

Why is the road to hell so broad? Jesus says "for the many who choose that way."

Heaven or hell? That's a choice *WE* make. We either follow God's truth about the way to heaven or we don't. It's that simple.

A few verses later, Jesus tells us exactly who's going to heaven. Listen carefully to what He says:

> Not everyone who calls out to me, "Lord! Lord!" will enter the Kingdom of Heaven. Only those who actually do the will of my Father in heaven will enter. — Matthew 7:21

> I am the way, the truth and the life. No one comes to the Father except through me.
> — John 14:6

Who's going to heaven? Jesus says, "Those who actually do the will of my Father in heaven will enter."

You might be asking, "Well, if God's such a loving God, then why would He create a place like hell?"

That's a great question, and Jesus actually gives us the answer:

> Then the King will turn to those on the left and say, "Away with you, You cursed ones, into the eternal fire prepared for the devil and his demons."   — Matthew 25:41

When Jesus spoke about hell and eternal fire, he often used the Greek word *Gehenna,* which actually refers to the trash dump just outside the walls of Jerusalem during His day. Hell is nothing more than a "dump" created for Satan and the angels who followed in his rebellion. They sinned against almighty God. Being holy, God cannot look upon or dwell with sin. So God created hell — a fiery trash heap — as punishment for Satan's rebellion.

When we fail to sincerely ask for God's forgiveness and accept His Son's sacrifice on the cross for our sins, we sin against God. If we never seek His forgiveness and allow God's Spirit to change us and give us a new heart to follow after God's will, we retain our sin and die with our sin. Being sinful when we die requires a loving yet holy God to send us to an eternal punishment for rejecting Him and His wonderful offer of eternal life.

If you'd like to receive Christ into your life right now, go to the very last page of this book and find out what you need to do. Do it now!

Jesus Discusses Satan

Jesus reveals some of Satan's covert tactics in His parable about the sower and the seed. Notice what Jesus says, then let's break it down so we can understand these evil strategies:

Now listen to the explanation of the parable about the farmer planting seeds: The seed that fell on the footpath represents those who hear the message about the Kingdom and don't understand it, then the evil one comes and snatches away the seed that was planted in their hearts. The seed on the rocky soil represents those who hear the message and immediately receive it with joy. But since they don't have deep roots, they don't last long. They fall away as soon as they have problems or are persecuted for believing God's word. The seed that fell among the thorns represents those who hear God's word, but all too quickly the message

is crowded out by the worries of this life and the lure of wealth, so no fruit is produced.
—Matthew 13:18-22

- First, he'll keep you from understanding or even desiring to understand God's Word, the Bible.

  The seed that fell on the footpath represents those who hear the message about the Kingdom and don't understand it. Then the evil one comes and snatches away the seed that was planted in their hearts. —Matthew 13:19

- Secondly, he'll create problems in your life so you feel disillusioned about God and His Word. Or he'll create persecution.

  The seed on the rocky soil represents those who hear the message and immediately receive it with joy. But since they don't have deep roots, they don't last long: They fall away as soon as they have problems or are persecuted for believing God's word. —Matthew 13:20-21

- Thirdly, he'll consume your life with work, kids, sports, and other activities that prevent you from having time for God.

  The seed that fell among the thorns represents those who hear God's word, but all too quickly the message is crowded out

by the worries of this life and the lure of
wealth, so no fruit is produced.
—Matthew 13:22

• Next, he'll blind you to the truth about God
and His ways. He'll get you to trust in your
own abilities and strength.

If the Good News we preach is hidden
behind a veil, it is hidden only from
people who are perishing. Satan, who
is the god of this world, has blinded the
minds of those who don't believe. They
are unable to see the glorious light of the
Good News. They don't understand this
message about the glory of Christ.
—2 Corinthians 4:3-4

• He'll create problems in your life or marriage
that allow you to eventually turn your mind
away from God.

The seed on the rocky soil represents
those who hear the message and immediately receive it with joy. But since they
don't have deep roots, they don't last
long. They fall away as soon as they have
problems or are persecuted for believing
God's word.   —Matthew 13:18

• He'll preoccupy your life with so much
stuff, you'll be too busy to have a relationship with God (Matthew 13:22).

Sadly, I often talk to many parents who are so busy running their kids to soccer games, football games, cheerleading, and other events that they barely have any alone time at all – especially with God. Americans are especially prone to this habit. We compress way too much into a twenty-four-hour period, especially weekends. Many people are so physically spent by Saturday night, the whole idea of church on Sunday is an afterthought—or not a thought at all.

This is just part of Satan's game plan:

- He'll blind people's spiritual eyes so they can't see the truth of the gospel of Jesus Christ (2 Corinthians 4:3-4).
- He'll get them enslaved to the things of this world so that they love this world more than they love God (Ephesians 2:1-3).
- He'll oppress people with pride, lust for money, lust for power, lust for a position, or an addiction such as alcohol, drugs, sex, etc. (Romans 1:22-25).
- He'll enslave world leaders and influencers to his will to destroy entire races of people by the millions (Daniel 10).

3. Corruption in the church scheme

While persecuting God's church will always be a part of what Satan does, he does it so subtly.

First he'll infiltrate the church with false believers. It happened in the early church shortly after Jesus ascended into heaven. The apostle Paul spoke of it in the book of Galatians:

Even that question came up only because of
some so-called believers there — false ones,
really — who were secretly brought in. They
sneaked in to spy on us and take away the
freedom we have in Christ Jesus.

—Galatians 2:4

False Christians are like cancer to the body of
Christ. They're more interested in their agenda
than God's. They'll start rumors about others,
create division within the church, fight over small
and insignificant issues, and end up disheartening
people in the church. They'll suck the joy right out
of a great ministry. It usually starts as an attack on
the pastoral leadership.

False teachers will also infiltrate the church.

I'll never forget the damage done to our large
church when I was a kid. A missionary from
Thailand was invited to become the pastor of our
church, and the church members cast their ballots
to support him. About a year into his tenure, he
started teaching that the Bible was a mere book of
stories symbolizing truth. That included Adam and
Eve. To this pastor, they were just a myth.

This statement shook many people to the core.
Many left the church, including my dad, who was
chairman of the deacons at the time.

Satan loves to create divisions within the
church. He will sneak up and use anybody who's
unsuspecting. False believers and false teachers
don't care if the church divides. They just want to
get their way.

The Bible promotes the opposite. It calls out for
unity and urges us to make every effort to preserve
unity within the body:

Make every effort to keep yourselves united in the Spirit, binding yourselves together with peace.   — Ephesians 4:3

Chapter 12

Angels in the Last Days

As we approach the last days before the coming of Christ, God's angels will have an important role in His attempt to bring *ALL* people to Christ. In doing so, they will become God's avengers to help Him bring judgment to the earth. These judgments are designed to get man's attention. They will prove God's existence, His power, His authority, and His great desire that people should live holy before Him.

As we look through the pages of the Bible, we see how God often uses angels when destroying cities or aiding in the judgment of nations. In the passage below, King David of Israel notes how God used a band of "destroying angels" to devour Egypt during the time when Moses led the children of Israel out of Egypt.

Throughout the pages of the Bible, God shows us how He has used angels to do the following events:

Punish wicked nations

He loosed on them his fierce anger—all his fury, rage, and hostility. He dispatched against them a band of destroying angels.

—Psalm 78:49

Punish the unfaithfulness of God's children

So the LORD sent a plague upon Israel, and 70,000 people died as a result. And God sent an angel to destroy Jerusalem. But just as the angel was preparing to destroy it, the LORD relented and said to the death angel, 'Stop! That is enough!' At that moment, the angel of the LORD was standing by the threshing floor of Araunah the Jebusite. David looked up and saw the angel of the LORD standing between heaven and earth with his sword drawn, reaching out over Jerusalem.

—1 Chronicles 21:14-16

Silence those who are arrogant

When the day arrived, Herod put on his royal robes, sat on his throne and made a speech to them. The people gave him a great ovation, shouting, 'It's the voice of a god, not of a man!' Instantly, an angel of the Lord struck Herod with a sickness because he accepted the people's worship instead of giving the glory to God. So he was consumed with worms and died.   — Acts 12:21-23

Destroy all who disobey

> And God will provide rest for you who are
> being persecuted and also for us when the
> Lord Jesus appears from heaven. He will
> come with his mighty angels in flaming
> fire, bringing judgment on those who don't
> know God and on those who refuse to obey
> the Good News of our Lord Jesus.
>
> —2 Thessalonians 7-8)

What part will angels play in the "last days"?

In the book of Revelation, angels play a predominant role. From preaching the gospel to binding Satan into the bottomless pit, angels are heavily involved in the "end time" program God is sending on earth. Their role becomes more apparent during the last seven years before Christ returns to rule in Jerusalem.

As we read Revelation, we can see angels doing a variety of things:

- An angel sealing the forehead of those who give their lives to God.
- An angel proclaiming the gospel of Christ.
- An angel announcing the fall of Babylon.
- Angels witnessing the Antichrist's torment in the Lake of Fire.
- Angels harvesting the true believers.
- An angel who beckons the birds to eat flesh at Armageddon.
- An angel who binds Satan and casts him into the bottomless pit.
- Angels who stand guard over the New Jerusalem.

While all these angels serve important roles, probably none are more significant than the seven angels known as "the seven angels of the apocalypse."

The Seven Angels of the Apocalypse

It's widely believed that the seven angels who bring unprecedented destruction upon earth are the archangels of God. Many scholars believe these are the angels that open the seven seals, blow the seven trumpets, and empty the seven bowls—each having some type of destructive force or significant purpose.

While the Bible doesn't tell us it's the archangels that specifically do these things, it's assumed that these special angels have tremendous authority and significance in the presence of God. In addition, their actions are warlike in manner—a similar trait to the nature of archangels.

If you remember from the previous chapters, angels vary in responsibility and strength. God has also ranked them, placing the archangels as chief among them all.

Some theologians try to classify angels into three general categories:

1. Those who worship
2. Those who are messengers and deal with mankind
3. Those who engage in battle with Satan and the fallen angels

I think some, if not all angels, are involved in all three of these events!

Daniel 10:12-21 is a case in point. According to Daniel, one specific angel in God's presence delivered an answer to Daniel's prayer as he was worshipping God. That same angel was both a messenger and a warrior. Notice how he brings a message to Daniel *and* tells him to return and fight against spirit princes:

Then he said, "Don't be afraid, Daniel. Since the first day you began to pray for understanding and to humble yourself before your God, your request has been heard in heaven. I have come in answer to your prayer. But for twenty-one days the spirit prince of the kingdom of Persia blocked my way. Then Michael, one of the archangels, came to help me, and I left him there with the spirit prince of the kingdom of Persia. Now I am here to explain what will happen to your people in the future, for this vision concerns a time yet to come.

Then in verses 20-21 he's a warrior:

He replied, "Do you know why I have come? Soon I must return to fight against the spirit prince of the kingdom of Persia, and after that the spirit prince of the kingdom of Greece will come. Meanwhile, I will tell you what is written in the Book of Truth. (No one helps me against these spirit princes except Michael, your spirit prince.

In this passage, you can easily see that this angel did all three. He was in Heaven worshipping God as he stood in His Presence. As Daniel prayed, the angel was given a message by God to bring to Daniel. After delivering the message, he admits that he must return to fight against the spirit prince of Persia.

Therefore, it seems to me that angels serve in all three capacities: to worship before God, to bring messages from God, and to fight against other spirits.

The Angels of the Seven Seals, Seven Trumpets, and Seven Bowls?

It's very clear from Scripture that there are seven angels who are involved in leading the way as God pours out His judgment on the earth and on mankind. Many theologians and Jewish leaders believe these seven angels are the seven archangels – angels of the highest rank. In the book of Revelation, these seven angels open seven seals, blow seven trumpets, and pour out seven bowls – all of which represent some kind of catastrophic event poured out upon the earth and upon man.

The seven seals (Revelation 6:1-17, 8:1-5), seven trumpets (Revelation 8:6-13, 11:15-19), and seven bowls/vials (Revelation 16:1-21) are a succeeding series of end-time judgments from God. These judgments get progressively worse and more devastating as the end times get closer. The seven seals, trumpets, and bowls are connected to each other whereas the seventh seal introduces the seven trumpets, and the seventh trumpet introduces the seven bowls.

The first four of the seven seals are known as the four horsemen of the Apocalypse. The first seal introduces the Antichrist (Revelation 6:1-2). The second seal causes great warfare (Revelation 6:3-4). The third seal causes famine (Revelation 6:5-6). The fourth seal brings about plague, further famine, and more warfare (Revelation 6:7-8).

The fifth seal reveals who will be martyred for their faith in Christ during the end times (Revelation 6:9-11). When the sixth of the seven seals is broken, a devastating earthquake occurs, causing massive upheaval and terrible devastation along with unusual astronomical phenomena (Revelation 6:12-14). According to the Bible, those who survive will cry out, "Fall on us and hide us from the face of him who sits on the throne and from the wrath of the Lamb! For the great day of their wrath has come, and who can stand?" (Revelation 6:16-17).

The seven trumpets are described in Revelation 8:6-13 as the "contents" of the seventh seal (Revelation 8:1-5). The first trumpet causes hail and fire, destroying one-third of all plant life in the world (Revelation 8:7). The second trumpet warns of a meteor or perhaps a nuclear bomb striking the oceans, causing the death of one-third of the world's sea life (Revelation 8:8-9). The third trumpet is similar to the second except it affects the world's lakes and rivers, causing all drinking water to become bitter (Revelation 8:10-11).

The fourth of the seven trumpets causes the sun and moon to dim, causing an unusual darkness over the earth (Revelation 8:12). The fifth trumpet results in a plague of "demonic locusts" that attack and torture humanity (Revelation 9:1-11). The sixth trumpet releases a demonic army that kills one-third of humanity (Revelation 9:12-21). The seventh trumpet calls forth the seven angels with the seven bowls of God's wrath (Revelation 11:15-19, 15:1-8).

The Worst Is Yet to Come!

So you think what you've just read is horrible? Think again. There's still more of God's wrath coming. As bad as it's gotten, millions upon millions of people all over the world will *still* refuse to humble themselves before God and receive Christ. In spite of God's chastening, man is hell-bent on rejecting God. It's absolutely unbelievable to me just how sinful, arrogant, and spiritually blind we human beings are.

As the angels pour out their bowls, the first bowl (Revelation 16:2) attacks those who bear the mark of the beast—the number 666—on their forehead or right hand. This bowl initiates a terrible plague upon those who have the mark of the Antichrist. The second bowl (Revelation 16:3) causes everything in the sea to die. The third bowl (Revelation 16:4) allows drinking water to turn to blood, thus causing mankind to scramble for something to quench his thirst.

The fourth bowl (Revelation 16:8-9) speaks of a heatwave that will burn people all over the world. This could mean solar flares or something of that nature. The fifth bowl (Revelation 16:10-11) causes the destruction of the Antichrist and his empire. The sixth bowl (Revelation 16:12-14) represents imprisoned demonic spirits set free for a period of time to gather all the armies of the world together to fight against God in the battle of Armageddon in the Valley of Megiddo. It's estimated that some four hundred million troops will not only gather in the Valley of Megiddo, but will spread out over a two-hundred-mile stretch of land that encompasses the Valley of Esdraelon, the Valley of Jehoshaphat, and Bozrah.

The seventh bowl (Revelation 16:17-21) will be the destruction of all these armies and a worldwide upheaval. There will also be a series of devastating earthquakes throughout the region, causing mass destruction like man has never seen.

As horrific as all this sounds, man will *still* reject God. This proves his sinful nature and arrogance. Man is simply so stubborn, he's ignorant. Many of the people who think Christians are delusional will one day conclude they were the ones who were delusional. The entire world will live in fear unlike any other time in history.

> Every arm is paralyzed with fear. Every heart melts, and people are terrified. Pangs of anguish grip them, like those of a woman in labor. They look helplessly at one another, their faces aflame with fear. For see, the day of the LORD is coming—the terrible day of his fury and fierce anger. The land will be made desolate, and all the sinners destroyed with it. The heavens will be black above them; the stars will give no light. The sun will be dark when it rises, and the moon will provide no light. 'I, the LORD, will punish the world for its evil and the wicked for their sin. I will crush the arrogance of the proud and humble the pride of the mighty.   —Isaiah 13:7-11

By the time the seventh angel pours out the seventh bowl of catastrophic events, all of mankind will finally drop to their knees in utter surrender to God. While all may seem bleak, this is actually the beginning of "heaven on earth"!

Everything on Earth Will Change

The seven years of the Great Tribulation will take human drama to its highest level in history. But it's nothing compared to the changes Jesus Christ will make when He returns to earth. With His saints, He will rule the earth for a thousand years. This will be the actual physical return, rule, and reign of Jesus Christ on earth. In fact, this millennial reign is really the fulfillment of God's dream—to dwell in sweet fellowship with His people.

Jesus prayed for this millennial reign and encouraged us to pray for it as well. In the famous prayer many people call "The Lord's Prayer" found in Matthew 6:9-13, He speaks of it when He says, "Thy kingdom come. . ."

The reign of Christ on earth has been promised since the beginning of man, and it's supported many times throughout the Bible. In fact, more than 25 percent of the Bible is about prophetic events. And most of that 25 percent covers the reign of Christ on earth for a thousand years.

There are many names given to the millennial reign of Christ in the Bible:

- The day of vengeance (Isa. 63:4)
- The regeneration (Matt.19:28)
- The restitution of all things (Acts 3:21)
- The times of refreshing (Acts 3:19)
- The world to come (Heb. 2:5)
- The kingdom of heaven (Matt. 5:10)

- The kingdom of God (Mark 1:14)
- The last day (John 6:40)
- The day of Christ (1 Cor. 1:8, 5:5; 2 Cor. 1:14; Phil. 1:6, 2:16)

The thousand-year reign of Jesus Christ will begin with the same last words He uttered on the cross just before He died. As the armies of the earth come against Israel to destroy her, a thunderous voice will project forth from the Temple saying, "It is finished!" In fact, it will be so loud it will shake both the earth and things in heaven. This will cause the earth and the heavens to experience a tremendous upheaval as mountains all over the world are leveled and islands suddenly disappear.

> Then the seventh angel poured out his bowl into the air. And a mighty shout came from the throne in the Temple, saying, 'It is finished!' Then the thunder crashed and rolled, and lightning flashed. And a great earthquake struck—the worst since people were placed on the earth. The great city of Babylon split into three sections, and the cities of many nations fell into heaps of rubble. So God remembered all of Babylon's sins, and He made her drink the cup that was filled with the wine of His fierce wrath. And every island disappeared, and all the mountains were leveled. There was a terrible hailstorm, and hailstones weighing as much as seventy-five pounds fell from the sky onto the people below. They cursed God because of the terrible plague of the hailstorm.
> —Revelation 16:17-21

When God spoke from Mount Sinai, His voice shook the earth, but now He makes another promise: 'Once again I will shake not only the earth but the heavens also.' This means that all of creation will be shaken and removed, so that only unshakable things will remain.   —Hebrews 12:26-27

This event was prophesied in the book of Isaiah many centuries before.

For I will shake the heavens. The earth will move from its place when the Lord of Heaven's Armies displays His wrath in the day of His fierce anger.   —Isaiah 13:13

In this verse, the angels are referred to as "Heaven's Armies." Angels will play a key role in future events as they relate to end times and the second coming of Christ.

Angels Capture the Beast and False Prophet

After Jesus blinds the 400-million-man army marching against Israel and slays all of them, the Bible says the spilling of blood will be so great it will flow through the Valley of Megiddo, the Valley of Jehoshaphat, and the Valley of Esdraelon as high as a horse's bridle, according to John.

The devastation will be so instantaneous and so great, we see an angel who will be given authority by God to command vultures from all over the world to feast upon the bodies of the slain troops (Revelation 19:17-20). The Bible says the vultures will literally gorge themselves upon the bodies of men.

> And I saw an angel standing in the sun, who cried in a loud voice to all the birds flying in midair, 'Come, gather together for the great supper of God, so that you may eat the flesh of kings, generals, and the mighty, of horses and their riders, and the flesh of all people, free and slave, great and small...' And the vultures all gorged themselves on the dead bodies.   —Revelation 19:17-18, 21

Immediately after the destruction of the 400 million-man army, another angel will capture the beast and the false prophet and throw them alive into the Lake of Fire.

> And the beast was captured, and with him the false prophet who did mighty miracles on behalf of the beast—miracles that deceived all who had accepted the mark of the beast and who worshiped his statue. Both the beast and his false prophet were thrown alive into the fiery lake of burning sulfur.   —Revelation 19:20

God is angry at their sinful ways. He shows them no mercy when they are thrown alive into the Lake of Fire.

Next on the agenda is the capture of Satan. A mighty angel, possibly one of the archangels, will capture Satan, bind him with a heavy chain, and cast him into "the bottomless pit" (or abyss) for a thousand years.

And I saw an angel coming down out of heaven, having the key to the Abyss and holding in his hand a great chain. He seized the dragon, that ancient serpent, who is the devil, or Satan, and bound him for a thousand years. He threw him into the Abyss, and locked and sealed it over him, to keep him from deceiving the nations anymore until the thousand years were ended.

—Revelation 20:1-3

As Jesus sets His foot upon the Mount of Olives just outside the Eastern Gate of Jerusalem, the mountain will split in two. This will mark the beginning of some major changes on earth. Jesus will clean house and issue a new way of living here on earth.

Jesus Will One Day Make Everything New

When Jesus comes to earth to set up His earthly kingdom, several things will change in a major way.

A new light

First, Jesus will have shaken the earth and heavens so terribly that Planet Earth will rotate off its axis. The sources of light we've known for centuries will cease to shed light on earth. As difficult as this may be to comprehend, I think the prophet Zechariah said it best:

Then the LORD my God will come, and all his holy ones with him. On that day the sources of light will no longer shine, yet there will be continuous day! Only the LORD knows how this could happen. There will be no normal day and night, for at evening time it will still be light. — Zechariah 14:5-7

A new government

There will be no need for politicians any longer! Jesus will rule on the Throne of David in Jerusalem, and all the earth will worship Him for the first time in history. Jesus will be king!

If you're a Christian, you will rule and reign with Christ. There won't be a need for any other government or political office. Jesus will rule the world and demand we live holy lives before Him. As a Christian, you will be given authority to rule over territories and peoples. Everything will be under His control.

And the LORD will be king over all the earth. On that day there will be one Lord — his name alone will be worshiped. — Zechariah 14:9

A new topography around the globe

The largest earthquake ever to hit our planet will happen when Jesus shouts at His coming (Revelation 16:17-21). Imagine that. The sound of His voice will change life as we know it. His voice will immediately destroy a 400-million-man army, ripple the earth in one massive earthquake, cause islands to disappear, and level mountains all over the world!

The end of religion as we know it

No longer will mankind have multiple religious faiths. There will be only one. It will be based solely on the worship of Jesus Christ as the Son of God. Jesus will provide a total spiritual makeover. With Satan bound in the bottomless pit, the sinful nature of man will be less prompted to sin. Jesus will sit on the Throne of David in Jerusalem, and believers in Christ will rule and reign with Him. He will be worshipped by all the nations of the world (Zechariah 14:9).

A new world attitude will prevail

Out of the prophecies of Isaiah (chapter 65), we see that a new attitude will prevail over the world. Here are a few of the things you'll find in Isaiah as well as other books of the Bible that speak of this particular time:

- extreme joy
- total peace
- a perfect society
- a fuller knowledge of God
- real happiness
- no sickness
- longevity of life
- economic prosperity
- agricultural prosperity
- a unified language
- unified worship
- increased light in the world
- the abiding presence of God

As we Christians reign with Christ, one of our responsibilities will be serving as judges over matters around the globe. The Lord Jesus will use us to serve Him to assure righteousness and justice.

Don't you realize that someday we believers will judge the world?   —1 Corinthians 6:2

The world will be in perfect bliss until the end of the thousand-year reign of Christ. When Christ's millennial reign comes to an end, God will allow Satan to be released from the bottomless pit for a short period. Once again, Satan will send his demons throughout the world to corrupt mankind after worshipping Jesus all these years.

True to form, man's arrogance and sinful nature will give in to temptation. Satan will recruit millions of people to his rebel army. But just as he forms his army, God the Father will shout from heaven and destroy his entire army. God's judgment will begin (Revelation 20:7-9).

Satan Cast into the Lake of Fire

Before God begins His final judgment—the Great White Throne Judgment—He will call to His angelic host to finally end Satan's reign and cast him into the Lake of Fire, where he will be tormented day and night throughout eternity.

Then the devil, who had deceived them, was thrown into the fiery lake of burning sulfur, joining the beast and the false prophet. There they will be tormented day and night forever and ever.   —Revelation 20:10

The Great White Throne Judgment

Every person who has ever lived (an estimated forty quadrillion) will stand before God to give account of his life as the angels look on (Revelation 20:11-15). Anyone whose name is not found recorded in the Book of Life will be thrown into the Lake of Fire.

The Judgment of Angels

While the Bible does not give us any clear indication of when the demons are judged, it's my assumption that it will happen during this time when God will give believers in Christ the opportunity to cast sentence on the demons who have plagued the world for centuries. In 1 Corinthians 6:2, the apostle Paul reminds believers that during the millennial reign, one of their responsibilities will be to serve Jesus Christ as righteous judges in civil matters all over the world.

In addition to judging mankind, we'll also be responsible for judging angels as well, according to Paul. Presumably, these are the fallen angels since they are the only ones that deserve judgment.

> And since you are going to judge the world, can't you decide even these little things among yourselves? ³ Don't you realize that we will judge angels? So you should surely be able to resolve ordinary disputes in this life.   —I Corinthians 6:2-3

During this time the demons will be absolutely terrified! It will be much like the time they cried out in horror when Jesus cast out demons in a couple of men who lived in a cemetery in the land of the Gadarenes. Listen to what they said:

> They began screaming at him, 'Why are you interfering with us, Son of God? Have you come here to torture us before God's appointed time?' —Matthew 8:29

A New Heaven and New Earth

It's hard to imagine, but after all these things God will start everything over. He will create a new heaven and a new earth. It will be far more beautiful and wonderful than the human mind can imagine.

As I think about it, I'm reminded of the scripture found in 1 Corinthians:

> No eye has seen, no ear has heard, and no mind has imagined what God has prepared for those who love him. —1 Corinthians 2:9

Chapter 13

Why Angels Stand Amazed

According to Fact Monster, there are more than 1.5 million known species of animals, insects, and plants that fill the earth with some 10,000 species of animals being discovered every year. In other words, with every year that passes, science discovers new things about our planet. We uncover new species and open the door to new revelations about our world we never knew existed.

Hopefully, reading of this book has prompted you to become more mindful of the world in which you live. Though much more could be said about angels, you've learned beyond the veil that separates the physical dimension from the spiritual dimension there is a world of spiritual beings who are just as active and busy as we are each day. It might seem a little scary, but you've learned how much God loves you and how He uses His angels to protect you and guide you. You've also learned how to defeat the onslaught of demonic forces who want to pull you down and away from God.

It's important for you to keep in mind: out of all the species God created the most important to

Him is man. It was man who was given the privilege to be created in the image of God. It was for man to which God created the angels. And it is for man that God sent His Son, Jesus Christ, to die and provide an opportunity to spend an eternity in Heaven with Him.

It's for these reasons that angels stand amazed at you and me. They are amazed at God's love for you. They are amazed how often He forgives you. They are amazed how patient he is with you. They are amazed that a Holy God doesn't destroy you the moment you lie, steal, cheat, or even kill. They are amazed at how God enjoys you in spite of your unwillingness to give Him much attention.

Angels are also amazed about your relationship to God and how you respond to the preaching of the gospel. Notice what 1 Peter 1:12 says,

And now this Good News has been announced to you by those who preached in the power of the Holy Spirit sent from heaven. It is all so wonderful that even the angels are eagerly watching these things happen.

Do you know what an angel's greatest hope is? It's to give your life to Christ!

What brings them more amazement than anything else is your willingness to give your life to Christ. The Bible says there is great rejoicing among the angels in Heaven when a sinner repents and gives their life to Christ.

So how do you give your life to Christ? How do you make sure you'll spend eternity in heaven with

God? How do you get the angels in Heaven excited about what you're doing?

It's by either giving your life to Christ, or by leading someone to Christ.

A man once asked me, "Do you really think you're going to heaven?"

To him I replied, "Yes, I do!"

He then responded with a question that sounded very reasonable, "Doesn't that sound a little arrogant or even naïve to actually think you're going to heaven? After all, what makes you so special that you would have such certainty about going there after you die?"

I assured him it had nothing to do with arrogance or because I have some "special" place with God. As a matter of fact, I told him I was a sinner just like him, and that I didn't think myself any more special than anyone else. What I did tell him was that I based my beliefs on what the Scriptures say about who's going to heaven and who's not.

He looked at me a little quizzically, having doubts about the meaning of my words. So I shared with him the following verses:

> And this is what God has testified: He has given us eternal life, and this life is in his Son. Whoever has the Son has life; whoever does not have God's Son does not have life. I have written this to you who believe in the name of the Son of God, so that you may know you have eternal life. —1 John 5:11-13

I then shared with him the meaning of this passage and how simple it is. It defines for us some very important truths. First, that God has given us the gift of eternal life with Him in heaven. However, this passage also explains that eternal life only comes through His Son, Jesus Christ.

Secondly, I showed him verse 12, which clearly tells us that whoever has Jesus in their life is given the gift of eternal life. In contrast, it also shows us that whoever does *not* have Jesus does not have this eternal life that is so freely offered by God.

I summarized for this man that it is verse 13 that allows me to declare my confidence in going to heaven. The writer of this passage (John) tells us that we can know before we die if we're going to heaven or not.

You see, my belief in whether I'm going to heaven is not based on what I hope or some kind of self-concocted theory. It is based solely on whether I have invited Jesus into my life to become my Lord and Savior. It's based on the fact that I received Jesus Christ into my life, and that He is now the Lord of my life. On this basis alone does my faith rest. It is through this passage of Scripture (and many others) that I make the claim, "Yes, I'm going to heaven!"

The question is, "Can you say that?"

How to Make Sure You're Going to Heaven And How You Can Lead Someone To Christ

Let me provide you a simple way of receiving Christ into your life today. If you've already received Christ, here's a simple outline that you can follow to help someone else develop a relationship with Christ.

Follow this outline, then invite Jesus Christ to come into your life right now!

1. Confess to God that you're a sinner.

> There is none righteous, no, not one.
>
> —Romans 3:10

> For everyone has sinned; we all fall short of God's glorious standard.   —Romans 3:23

The fact is, we've all sinned against God. Whether it's a little white lie or something as simple as dishonoring our parents, it's all sin to God. Why? Because He's holy. He hates sin. It's the absolute opposite of His character. The very fact that He created hell for Satan and his demons should tell you just how much He hates sin. It's that bad!

As anyone with an addiction will tell you, the first step in finding healing is to admit your problem. At Alcoholics Anonymous meetings, for example, that's step #1. You must first confess you're an alcoholic. Like AA, the first step to having a right relationship with God is to admit you're a sinner.

2. Ask God to forgive you of your sins. Tell Him you want to turn away from your sins and begin living for Him.

> But if we confess our sins to him, he is faithful and just to forgive us our sins and to cleanse us from all wickedness.
>
> —1 John 1:9

Asking the Lord to forgive you of your sins is one thing, but repenting (or turning from your sin to God) is the action that proves to God you truly want forgiveness. Anyone can say, "Lord, I'm sorry for what I've done." In fact, many have said,

"Lord, forgive me for what I'm about to do." That's meaningless to God. Someone who is truly sorry for their sin turns away from their sinful ways and does everything they can to stop, trusting God to provide all the power they need.

Jesus once told the religious leaders of His day that they too needed to repent of their sins or they wouldn't go to heaven.

> No, and I tell you again that unless you repent, you will perish, too.   —Luke 13:5

3. Invite Jesus to become the Lord of your life.

God loves us so much that He gave His only Son, Jesus Christ, to die on a cross for the sins we committed. He paid the price for sin. God knew we could *NEVER* be good enough or holy enough to get into heaven. So He sent His Son to die in our place. Instead of us paying the price for sin—eternal death in hell—Jesus took our sins upon Himself as our substitute. He did this because He loves us so much, and as a gift to us. Jesus is the most precious gift of all.

Imagine the price Jesus paid for your sins! When He shed His blood for you on the cross, He paid the price for ALL your sins. All you have to do is invite Him to become the Lord of your life. That's it!

Then begin living for Him.

When you do this, guess what the angels will be doing? Partying it up big time!

> There is joy in the presence of God's angels when even one sinner repents. —Luke 15:10

In conclusion

Hopefully, as you've read this book, you've gained some powerful insights as to what's going on in the world around you. God has given us a lot of information about angels in His Word because He wants us to know about them. I would recommend that you re-read this book again and again.

I have a friend who owns a Taco Via restaurant here in the Kansas City area. For Christmas, her husband purchased her a set of my CD's on angels: a 5-disc series with an hour's worth of information on each disc.

One day I decided to grab me one of their delicious taco burgers. After ordering my food she mentioned that her husband had bought the CD's for her for Christmas and she had listened to all 5 discs at least 5 times. I wasn't quite sure I heard her correctly so I asked her, "Did you say that you listened to all 5 discs, or that you listened to all 5 discs, five times?"

She smiled and said, "Right. I've listened to every disc 5 times."

I couldn't believe it. I jokingly responded and said, "If you've listened to all 5 discs, five times – then you're probably more of an expert on angels than I am!"

She laughed, and then shared with me how much she learned each time she listened to the disc.

I want to challenge you to do the same. Angels and demons are real. They are involved in our lives whether we like it or not. When we are mindful of their existence and consider how they operate from day to day, we can make better adjustments in life.

I sincerely hope you've learned a lot from this book. And, I hope you'll begin to take advantage of the information contained in this book to be like the angels:

- To obey God implicitly!
- To worship God enthusiastically!
- And, to serve Him ecstatically!

Next step – Write me!

Let me know how this book has helped you or if you have any questions—especially if you've given your life to Christ! **And, go to my website and tell me your angel story if you have one!**

www.AngelsUTM.com